C000102524

CONTENTS

ITALIAN COOKING

by

Robin Howe

INTRODUCTION

ITALIAN cooking is Mediterranean cooking and for many people Mediterranean cooking at its best. It is not complicated, much of it is distinctly earthy, so it allows itself to be reproduced in many parts of the world.

Those who judge Italian cooking carelessly claim that it is all spaghetti, garlic, olive oil and tomatoes, a claim which considerably annoys the Italians and is not even half true. Those foreigners who go to Italy without doing some culinary homework can be persuaded that Italian cooking is all spaghetti or noodles, but this is because so many of them, unable to speak Italian, are baffled by the menu and are far too shy to ask the waiter (who is usually all too willing to advise), so that they end by settling for familiar spaghetti and tomato sauce. And remember that, although it is possible to get any amount of pasta dishes throughout Italy, in the north rice is generally preferred.

There are two distinct cooking cultures in this country of extremely individual cooking: one, the wine-and-olive school, and, two, the milk-and-butter school. It is simply a matter of what grows where. Garlic is favoured in most regions but it is seldom used excessively; in Tuscany onions are used far more than garlic. Tomatoes reign supreme in southern Italy— but it is difficult to conceive of any Italian cooking without a tomato lurking in some corner or other.

Buy Italian pasta whenever you can. This is not propaganda but commonsense. Pasta is an Italian product. In Italy a great many small shops make fresh pasta of all kinds daily, which is quite delicious; and now in Britain, in areas where there is an Italian community, fresh noodle pastry and ravioli is often available on certain days of the week.

Meat, generally speaking, is expensive in Italy and in some parts of the country not all that good. This has resulted in an immense diversity of meat dishes and the wholesale use of offal of all kinds. Some exceedingly good dishes are made with tripe, liver, kidneys, even the spleen and lungs. Much of the meat is boiled or cut into small pieces, both for easier cooking (in a country which until recently did not have many home ovens), also to tenderize the meat; or it is left to simmer for hours in a mixture of vegetables, often tomatoes, or in red wine until it falls from the bone. Chicken, poultry and game also appear in many guises and in some areas roast pig on a spit is sold in the markets and public squares.

Fish is important—naturally, in a country where so many people live within a few miles of the sea—with plenty of exotic kinds as well as fish of a more everyday British nature. But in Britain today, too, the variety of fish is improving. Per-haps because of the increasingly cosmopolitan nature of our population we find cuttlefish, squid, octopus, red mullet, fresh sardines, and even anchovies, as well as salt cod, not only in the large London speciality shops, but in a great many out-of-the-way fishmongers, and in the deep freezes of many a village shop. Even when the original fish is not available, an Italian dish is still possible. Sprats or smelts can be used instead of sardines, for example; and halibut for tunny or swordfish. The flavour is quite different, but at least you will have learned a new way of cooking halibut.

An important feature of Italian cooking is the use of sauces, which are served with meat, fish and vegetables, as well as the numerous pasta dishes. Cheese also appears in numerous recipes but is always used with care for, as the Italians say, too much 'will spoil the touch of the food on the tongue'.

Another important ingredient in Italian cooking is wine, often added with a lavish hand. There are the everyday local wines, good for drinking and cooking, and which are cheap in Italy.

Although the Italians have a vast repertoire of sweet dishes, mouth-watering cakes and pastries (usually purchased from the shop down the road), they are seldom served to finish a meal; instead they eat fruit, always fruit in season, and what they are pleased to call *macedoine*—in other words, chopped fruit laced with local wines or liqueurs. Another favourite is pears served with cheese, in particular Parmesan which, when eaten fresh, is one of the finest cheeses in the world. For cooking it is matured until hard enough to grate. It is possible to buy chunks of grating Parmesan cheese in Britain.

The order of an Italian meal is somewhat similar to our own, except that the Italian likes to start with an *antipasto*, which can be anything: for instance, a paper-thin slice of *prosciutto*, or smoked ham, served alone or wrapped round a wedge of sweet melon or with fresh figs, a dish of cooked vegetables, or a plate of spaghetti. In other words, Italians do not start their meal with the main course and they most certainly do not consider that a dish of spaghetti or other pasta constitutes a meal. (The foreigner ordering pasta as a first course might be wise to ask for a half portion.)

Soups are popular and varied, and these come both hot and cold, thick and thin. Some, like *risi e bisi*, are so thick they are eaten with a fork. Italian fish soups (*brodetto*) are served all round the long coastline and each fishing port claims to make the best.

After the *antipasto* comes the main course, usually served with a salad, almost never with cooked vegetables, since these are considered a dish in their own right.

On the whole Italians do not drink hard liquor. They have their wines, aperitifs and liqueurs; usually they drink wine with their meals but few Italians will drink wine on an empty stomach.

To add a short note on ingredients used in Italian cooking; fortunately today even the smallest shop has foreign foods of all kinds, so it is not difficult to find the ingredients required to make authentic-tasting Italian dishes. Even so, a little advice might be of use to the newcomer in this field.

Olive oil has a distinctive taste and differs not only from country to country but also from region to region. Therefore, when preparing Italian dishes do try to find Italian olive oil. Not because it is any better but simply for its particular flavour. Also I prefer to use Italian tinned tomatoes for Italian dishes, again simply because their flavour is so different from our own. This also applies to tomato paste.

Ricotta cheese is not so easily found, except in Italian shops, so use plain, not creamy, cottage cheese when ricotta is not available. Italian salami or mortadella are sausages which are generally available, but *prosciutto* or finely-sliced Italian ham is not. This is expensive even in Italy. A substitute for it could be paper-thin slices of smoked bacon.

Olives and anchovies are usually available loose in delicatessen stores or Italian shops, and are cheaper and rather stronger in taste than those in jars. All butter should be unsalted. Italian wines have their own particular aroma and taste, and should not be difficult to find. Mozzarella cheese is usually available in Italian shops; otherwise substitute with Bel Paese.

It is probably easier to become an 'expert' in Italian cooking than it is in any other kind, and it is certainly almost impossible to avoid becoming an enthusiast.

SEASONING,
HERBS AND SPICES

IN THIS list only those spices and herbs have been given which are more generally used in Italy and which are available as a rule in England. Whenever possible it is obviously better to use fresh herbs, but for the Londoner this is not always possible, even in these days of window-box gardening.* If you are not used to herbs and spices in cooking, start by being over-cautious; they should add a subtle flavour to a dish, and not drown other tastes. After a time you will discover that herbs rightly used become something personal in your cooking and that most dishes, even tried favourites, gain something with the addition of herbs.

ANISEED (*Anice*)
The young fresh leaves are good in salads, while the seeds are often put into cakes, pastries, and cottage cheese dishes.

BASIL (*Basilico*)
One of the most popular herbs in Italian cooking. Use it fresh in salads, ragouts, stews, savoury dishes, sauces, soups, bisques. Strongly flavoured, the sweet variety is most favoured. Can be used dried.

BAYLEAF (*Lauro*)
One leaf is usually enough to flavour a dish. Use in sauces, soups, stews, and most fish dishes.

BORAGE (*Borraggine*)
Use young leaves in salads. Italians make fritters with the firmer larger leaves.

* The following from among the herbs listed can be grown in window-boxes or pots: borage, fennel, marjoram, mint, parsley, sage, tarragon and thyme.

CAPERS (*Capperi*)
Extensively used in Italian cooking, especially with fish and vegetables.

CHILI PEPPERS (*Pepe forte*)
Small red peppers. Use with moderation when a hot pungent flavour is needed.

CINNAMON (*Cannella*)
Use the sticks whenever possible; the flavour is better and they can be used several times.

CLOVES (*Chiodo di garofano*)
Use both whole and ground, especially when flavouring meat and game dishes. Excellent in soups.

FENNEL (*Finocchio*)
Greatly favoured by the Italians, who grow the thick variety which looks a little like celery. Used in salads, and cooking generally, and the seeds as in England.

GARLIC (*Aglio*)
Use freely but wisely in almost all savoury and vegetable dishes.

MACE (*Scorza di Noce Moscata*)
Use in savoury dishes as well as sweet.

MARJORAM (*Maggiorana*)
Very popular in Italy where the sweet variety is preferred.

MINT (*Menta*)
Use in omelettes, stews, savoury dishes, also in salads but less often in sauce.

NUTMEG (*Noce Moscata*)
Use in meat and savoury dishes as well as in cakes, etc.

PAPRIKA
Use as a flavouring and as a garnish. Generally the sweet Hungarian variety is preferred. This is not hot, but has a pleasant almost sweet flavour.

PINE NUTS (*Pinoli*)
Very small white bullet-shaped nuts or kernels. Excellent with rice and other savoury dishes, typically Mediterranean.

PISTACHIO (*Pistacchio*)
Bright green nuts, used in cakes, sweets and ice creams.

OREGAN (*Origano*)
A variety of marjoram which is used in the same way.

PARSLEY (*Prezzemolo*)
Use in almost every savoury dish, especially when garlic has been included.

ROSEMARY (*Rosmarino*)
Use with poultry, fish and veal. Its somewhat bitter taste changes during cooking to a more delicate flavour.

SAFFRON (*Zafferano*)
A dull orange coloured spice. Use it for its flavour and its colour. Particularly good in savoury rice dishes. It is expensive but one only needs it in tiny quantities.

SAGE (*Salvia*)
The Italians love this herb and use it all the time.

TARRAGON (*Dragoncello*)
Use fresh, both for its flavour and decorative appearance. Excellent in soups, sauces, ragouts, etc.

THYME (*Timo*)
Use plentifully in all types of savoury dishes.

VANILLA (*Vaniglia*)
Use the pods, as their flavour is better than any essence. They can be used again and again.

HORS-D'OEUVRE

ANTIPASTO

ITALIAN *antipasto* is as regional as all Italian cooking and varies tremendously from the elegant and rather more formal approach of the Bolognese to the simple vegetables, olives, sweet peppers, etc, of the Sicilian.

Between these extremes one might say that 'anything goes' and that the housewife intent on giving an Italian meal may rest assured that within limits she cannot go wrong in presenting her first course if it consists of *antipasto*.

Although *antipasto* is an integral part of the Italian cuisine, many people dispense with this course nowadays and start with either a rice or a spaghetti dish, depending on whether they are from the North or South.

The recipes and suggestions given in this chapter are those more generally served, to the accompaniment of a typical mild Italian aperitif.

FISH

Filleted anchovies; sardines fried and stuffed; oysters served *au naturel* or on strips of bread previously spread with caviar; tinned tunny fish with slices of sweet peppers; any of the fish *fritto misto*; shrimps and prawns served either very simply with lemon juice or with salad cream.

EGGS

Hardboiled and sliced, garnished with anchovies or mayonnaise; devilled and baked, stuffed with various piquant mixtures.

HAM

Usually tangy flavoured *prosciutto* is used, always paper-thin sliced and served with green and purple figs, or spread with

14

honey. In the melon season it is served with thin slices of ice-cold green melon.

MEATS

Here the Italians excel and a plate of cold meats, all beautifully sliced and garnished with aspic, is a joy. It will include cold beef, cooked very rare; lamb and ham; pork and veal; sliced meat galantine; all kinds of piquant sausages, *salami* and the like; *mortadella* flavoured with pistachio nuts; in fact, almost every type of meat or sausage one is likely to meet.

MELON

In season this is very popular, served either with *prosciutto*, or quite plain sprinkled with sugar, or well soaked in wine. This is done by cutting off a small round at the top of the melon, scooping out all the seeds, and pouring in a glass of marsala or sherry. It is then almost frozen and served in small cubes.

SUNDRIES

Other suggestions are pickled mushrooms and onions, olives both green and black, cubes of tunny fish with red peppers, tomatoes raw and cooked, slivers of white cheese, tartlets with savoury fillings and garnished with anchovies or mayonnaise; small and large *pizze*, canapés smeared with mullet roe, smoked salmon, and home-made pastes, croquettes of spinach or meat, or of potato well flavoured with cheese.

CHEESE AND BLACK OLIVES
FRIED TOGETHER
FORMAGGIO CON OLIVE NERE

Cut four ounces of firm cheese (something of the bel paese type) into cubes and stone one dozen ripe black olives. Fry them together in butter until the cheese is blistered and amber coloured. Add a tablespoonful of white wine, bring to the boil and simmer for two minutes. Spread on buttered toast and sprinkle with black pepper.

FRIED CHEESE SLICES
CHIZZE CON FORMAGGIO

5 oz. flour	*1 egg*
1 oz. butter	*Pinch of salt*
4 oz. grated Parmesan cheese	*Olive oil for frying*

Sift the flour and salt together then rub in the butter. Mix with the egg and a little cold water to make a pastry. Leave for an hour. Roll out the pastry very thin, sprinkle generously with grated cheese, then pat the cheese into it. Cut the pastry into squares and fry in deep boiling oil until crisp and amber colour.

PARMESAN CHEESE BREAD FINGERS
CROSTINI ALLA PARMIGIANA

Cut several slices of stale white bread into fingers. Soak these for fifteen minutes in milk. Sprinkle with salt and pepper and thoroughly coat with grated Parmesan cheese. Pat the cheese well into the bread with the back of a wooden spoon, and fry the fingers in hot oil or butter until brown and crisp.

GREEN OLIVES, SICILIAN STYLE
OLIVE VERDI ALLA SICILIANA

Green olives immersed in cold water, salted and flavoured with fennel to taste. They should be left for several days.

FRIED MARROW, MILANESE STYLE
ZUCCHINI ALLA MILANESE

3 *courgettes*   *Breadcrumbs*
1 *to 2 beaten eggs*   *Salt and pepper*
Oil

Wash the marrows and cook them in boiling, salted water for fifteen minutes. Drain and cut them into quarter-inch thick slices. Cut off the skin. Dip the slices in beaten egg and coat with seasoned breadcrumbs. Fry in very hot oil until brown on both sides. Reduce the heat and simmer gently for five minutes.

STUFFED CUCUMBERS
CETRIOLI ALLA DUSE

2 *cucumbers*   1 *small onion*
8 *anchovy fillets*   2–3 *radishes*
2 *eggs*   *Olive oil*
1 *tablespoon vinegar*   *Tomato and lemon for garnish-*
Dried mustard   *ing*

Wash the cucumbers and cut off their ends. Slice them into lengths of about one and a half inches. Put them into boiling water, add the vinegar and cook them for just five minutes.

Boil the eggs until hard, chop and mash them until smooth. Mix with a teaspoonful of mustard, the onion, very finely chopped, the anchovy, well pounded, and the radishes, previously grated. Add enough olive oil to bind these ingredients. Scoop out the centres of the cucumber 'tubes', mix the centres with the egg mixture, and re-fill the cucumber pieces with it. Serve cold, surrounded by slices of raw tomato and wedges of lemon.

2

MARINATED COURGETTES
ZUCCHINI IN SALMI

1 *lb. courgettes*
Wine vinegar
Bayleaves, clove and pepper
1 *sliced onion*

1 *sliced carrot*
Salt and pepper
Oil for frying

Wash and slice the courgettes. Fry in hot oil until brown
on both sides. Cover and simmer for five minutes. Drain and
put into a flat dish.

Bring equal quantities of vinegar and water to the boil—
enough to cover the sliced courgette—and add the remaining
ingredients. Allow to cool then pour this marinade over the
courgettes. Leave for twenty-four hours.

DEVILLED EGGS
UOVA RIPIENE

6 *hardboiled eggs*
Salt and pepper
Onion juice to taste
Olive oil
¼ *pint béchamel sauce*

Capers
Anchovies
Gherkin
Chopped parsley

Cut the eggs into halves crosswise, then cut off the tips so that
they will stand upright. Scoop out the yolks and mix with salt,
pepper, a very little olive oil and onion juice. Mash until
smooth, then pile back into the whites. Garnish each egg with
capers, anchovies and gherkin. Arrange in a shallow casserole
and bake in a very slow oven for five minutes. Put on to a hot
dish, cover with hot béchamel sauce, sprinkle with chopped
parsley and serve hot.

STUFFED PEPPERS
PEPERONI RIPIENI

6 *large green peppers*   6 *chopped tomatoes*
4 *oz. white breadcrumbs*   12 *anchovies*
Handful parsley, chopped   ½ *cup cooked rice*
1 *clove garlic, chopped*   ¼ *cup oil*

Wash the peppers, neatly cut off the tops and scoop out the core and seeds. Drop in boiling water and cook for exactly three minutes.

Heat the oil and fry the garlic and breadcrumbs, add the tomatoes and simmer until these are soft. Add remaining ingredients and stir well. Fill the peppers with this mixture. Replace the tops of the peppers.

Put the peppers in a baking pan, cover the bottom with boiling water and bake in a moderate oven for fifteen to twenty minutes, or until the peppers are soft.

Remove the tops before serving and serve with tomato sauce (see page 196).

SPINACH DUMPLINGS
POLPETTINE DI SPINACI

1 *lb. cooked spinach*   3 *oz. butter*
½ *lb. cottage cheese*   *Salt and pepper*
2 *oz. grated Parmesan cheese*   *Pinch nutmeg*
2 *egg yolks*   1 *teaspoon sugar*
1 *oz. flour*   1 *tablespoon cream*

Heat the butter, add the flour and cook to a roux. Add the cream (taking great care that the pan is not too hot) and then the spinach. Stir well, remove from the heat and add the cottage cheese, Parmesan, seasonings, sugar and nutmeg. Blend well and bind with well beaten yolks. The mixture must be firm enough to roll into dumplings.

Have ready a large pan with boiling salted water. Roll the spinach mixture into dumplings the size of a walnut and drop them, one by one, into the boiling water. Poach them for five minutes, then take them out with a perforated spoon. Serve hot, generously sprinkled with grated cheese and with a tomato sauce (page 196).

These dumplings are equally good fried in hot butter or oil instead of being poached, and shaped as croquettes.

STUFFED BAKED TOMATOES
POMIDORO RIPIENI ALLA CASALINGA

8 *large tomatoes*	*salt and pepper*
6 *oz. cooked minced meat*	1 *onion, chopped*
1–2 *beaten eggs*	1 *carrot, chopped*
1 *oz. dried mushrooms*	1 *stick celery, chopped*
3 *oz. grated Parmesan cheese*	1 *teaspoon sugar*
2 *oz. soft breadcrumbs*	1 *clove garlic, chopped*
Handful chopped parsley	½ *cup olive oil*

Soak the mushrooms for twenty minutes, then wash well and chop finely. Wash the tomatoes, cut off the tops and scoop out the insides.

Heat the oil, fry the chopped vegetables, garlic, parsley, meat and mushrooms. Add salt, pepper and sugar, then simmer until the vegetables are soft. Remove from the heat, cool slightly, then add the beaten egg(s), breadcrumbs and cheese. Pile this mixture lightly into the tomato cases, sprinkle with a little more cheese and breadcrumbs and cover with the tomato tops. Place in a large baking tin, pour in boiling water and bake in a moderate oven for thirty minutes.

FLORENTINE TOAST
CROSTINI ALLA FIORENTINA

Toast or fry as many slices of bread as required. Keep hot.
Sauté in butter one small grated onion, some sliced chicken
livers and a handful of chopped parsley. Add two anchovies
and a wineglassful of white wine. Thicken the sauce with
cream or flour, sprinkle with salt, pepper and paprika pepper.
Cover the slices of toast with the chicken livers and sauce.

RICE 'TELEPHONE' CROQUETTES
SUPPLÌ DI RISO

A popular Roman *antipasto*. It is a type of rice croquette
filled with meat, onion, etc, and diced mozzarella cheese.
When the croquettes are eaten the cheese forms long strings or
telephone wires.

1 *lb. rice*	2 *oz. butter*
3 *oz. Parmesan cheese*	*Salt and pepper*
1 *tablespoon mushrooms,*	*Stock or water*
chopped	3 *beaten eggs*
1 *onion, chopped*	*Diced mozzarella*
2 *tablespoons bacon, chopped*	*Breadcrumbs and flour*
2 *oz. cooked meat, minced*	*Oil*

Cook the rice in plenty of salted boiling stock or water for
ten to fifteen minutes. Drain and mix with half the Parmesan
cheese and one well-beaten egg. Leave to cool and prepare the
filling.

Heat the butter and fry the onion, bacon, mushrooms and,
lastly, the meat. Mix to a paste, remove from the fire and add
the second egg, pepper and the rest of the Parmesan cheese.

Take one tablespoonful of rice, put it in the palm of your

hand and smooth it out with the back of a wooden spoon. Place a portion of the filling in the centre with a piece of diced mozzarella. Close your hand in such a way that the rice completely envelops the filling. Shape into croquettes, roll in flour, the third beaten egg and breadcrumbs. Fry in deep boiling oil until a golden brown and serve hot.

SPAGHETTI,
RICE AND NOODLES

PASTA E RISO

WHILE the South loves its *pasta* dishes the North prefers rice, and some northern Italians will tell you with the utmost scorn that *pasta* is not to be found in the North at all. This is not entirely true, but it is a fact that all the best rice dishes come from the North and almost every northern Italian would rather eat rice than spaghetti. So while the South is busy preparing its numerous *pastas* the North is turning out one risotto after another, and while these are not quite so various as the rival *pastas*, it would be possible to produce a slim volume of recipes for them and their accompanying sauces and garnishes.

Gnocchi and *polenta* are not loves of my own, but they are generally popular with Italians, and the Roman is immensely proud of his version of potato *gnocchi*, while the man from Venice boasts of his prowess with *polenta* (cornmeal). It would be possible to write a whole chapter on them, but I think that my Italian friends will agree that many of these doubtless famous recipes are variations on a theme.

Pasta is another matter, for Italy has an incredible number of *pasta* products. It is said that their names run into thousands, but the number of the different varieties is more likely to be about one hundred and fifty. Identical products carry different names in different regions, and this makes it rather puzzling for the foreign tourist intent on trying different forms of *pasta*.

Concerning the origin of *pasta* there are several legends. The Neapolitans declare that the name macaroni came from a Cardinal of their town who on being presented with it for the first time exclaimed in joy '*Ma caroni*' (the little dears). Another legend says that noodles, etc. came from China *via* an Italian sailor who had learnt the art of making and preparing them from a Chinese lady-love. Marco Polo, too, is credited with having brought a load of noodles back with him from his long travels, with other rather more valuable cargo.

Whatever their origin, there is seemingly no end to their shapes and sizes. Today even the more diligent Italian housewife will buy manufactured spaghetti, vermicelli, and even the minute *anolini* so popular in soups. A good housewife, however, often makes her *ravioli* at home, also the *manicotti*—little stuffed hats, sometimes called *cima*—and usually she makes her own *lasagne* (wide noodles) and *tagliatelle* (noodle or ravioli pastry) for special occasions.

Fillings and sauces for all these *pastas* are also legion. Most of them contain tomato, but there are exceptions even to this rule. Each district has its speciality—in fact the Italians go one better than this and have special sauces or fillings for Festivals and Holy Days, and these can be very rich indeed Cheese is almost (but not quite) always served with *pasta* dishes.

One pound of *pasta* or of rice will feed four people.

NOODLE PASTRY

TAGLIERINI

Sieve two pounds of flour with a good pinch of salt on to a pastry board. Make a hollow in the centre and break eight eggs into it. Using a wooden fork, stir the flour gently into the eggs until a perfectly smooth mass is formed. Knead this until it is pliable and then leave for thirty minutes before using.

NOODLES. Take the ball of dough and divide it into six pieces. Shape each piece into a ball and roll out to almost paper-thin rounds of equal size. Roll each round—like rolling for a Swiss roll—and cut them into strips, using a very sharp knife. The width of the strips depends on their later use, narrow for soup; medium for general use, and wide when making a dish of lasagne. But the width is really a matter of taste. The strips can be used at once or left to dry for a while.

To make green noodles, add just enough cooked and sieved spinach to give the pastry a pale green shade. Allow to dry ten minutes longer. It is worth the trouble of making flat noodles and noodle pastry at home as the flavour is so much better than the commercially produced noodles. It also takes only a matter of up to five minutes to boil fresh pasta until tender or *al dente*.

BUTTERED NOODLES
FETTUCCINE ALL' ALFREDO

1 *lb. noodles*   *Butter*   *Grated Parmesan cheese*

Cook the noodles in rapidly boiling salted water for eight to ten minutes. Drain and mix with plenty of fresh butter, which should not be melted beforehand. Serve with grated cheese.

BAKED GREEN NOODLES
WITH CHEESE
LASAGNE VERDI AL FORNO

1 *lb. wide green noodles*	*Grated Parmesan cheese*
½ *pint Béchamel sauce*	1 *small tin tomato paste*
1 *onion, chopped*	*Wineglass of white wine*
1 *carrot, chopped*	¼ *pint stock*
1 *stick celery, chopped*	*Salt and pepper*
4 *oz. minced cooked meat*	2 *tablespoons oil*

Heat the oil, brown the onion, carrot and celery, then the meat.

Dilute the tomato paste with the stock, add this to the meat and vegetables and simmer for fifteen minutes. Add the wine, salt and pepper and continue to cook until the vegetables are very soft.

Cook the noodles in rapidly boiling salted water for eight minutes. Drain and pat them dry, separating the strips. Well grease an oven casserole and cover the bottom with a layer of noodles. Spread this with meat and vegetables and a little béchamel sauce and sprinkle with grated Parmesan cheese. Cover with another layer of noodles and repeat these layers until all the ingredients are used up, ending with Parmesan.

Cook in a hot oven until the cheese has browned.

NOODLES AND POTATO WITH GARLIC SAUCE
TRENETTE COL PESTO ALLA GENOVESE

Boil half a pound of potatoes in their skins until soft. Drain, peel and slice thickly into rounds. Cook half a pound of noodles for eight minutes in rapidly boiling salted water. Drain and mix with the sliced potatoes. Pour over them some thinned pesto (page 192) and sprinkle liberally with grated Parmesan cheese. Serve immediately. This is a Genoese speciality.

STUFFED MACARONI
MACCHERONI RIPIENI ALLA TOSCANA

The macaroni used in this recipe is short and thick, and looks like sawn-up lengths of drainpipe. Cook it for ten minutes in rapidly boiling water and drain it carefully so that the pieces keep their shape. Allow it to cool sufficiently to handle.

Have ready a typical Italian meat stuffing (page 37). Push this filling into the macaroni tubes and arrange carefully in a large pan. Add stock to cover and cook for another five minutes. Serve with a tomato sauce and grated cheese.

MACARONI TIMBALE
TIMBALLO DI MACCHERONI

½ *lb. fine macaroni*
2 *oz. butter*
1 *oz. flour*
1 *small grated onion*
4 *chicken livers*
3 *tablespoons brandy*

1 *sweetbread, sliced*
½ *pint stock*
2 *oz. dried mushrooms, soaked and chopped*
Salt and pepper

Boil the macaroni until almost tender in plenty of boiling salted water. Grease a timbale mould and line it with the macaroni.

Heat the butter and lightly brown the onion. Add the flour, stir and simmer for two minutes, then add the stock, salt, pepper, sliced sweetbread and chicken livers and mushrooms. Simmer all together for ten minutes, then add the brandy and pour this sauce into the centre of the timbale. Bake in a moderate oven for thirty minutes.

MACARONI, NEAPOLITAN STYLE
MACCHERONI ALLA NAPOLETANA

1 *lb. macaroni*
2 *lb. tomatoes*
1 *onion, chopped*
1 *stick celery, chopped*
1 *carrot, chopped*
4 *oz. diced fat bacon*

1 *oz. butter*
Salt and pepper
2 *sprigs basil*
1 *teaspoon sugar*
½ *cup oil*
Parmesan cheese, grated

Wash, peel and slice the tomatoes. Heat the oil with the bacon and brown the onion, celery and carrot. Add salt, pepper and basil, then the tomatoes. Simmer for five minutes, cover with water and continue to simmer for another forty minutes. Stir and add the butter and sugar. While the sauce is cooking, cook the maracroni in boiling salted water until tender but still firm. Drain in a colander and turn into a deep serving dish. Rub the sauce through a sieve, reheat, and pour it over the macaroni. Serve with grated Parmesan cheese.

BAKED MACARONI
MACCHERONI AL FORNO

Use the rather large macaroni for this dish and cook it in plenty of boiling salted water until it is just tender but not soft. Over-cooking turns it soggy.

1 *lb. large macaroni*	*Salt and pepper*
4 *oz. chopped mushrooms*	*Grated Parmesan cheese*
4 *sliced tomatoes*	*Butter and olive oil*
Handful of chopped parsley	½ *pint Béchamel sauce*

Heat equal parts of oil and butter and brown the tomatoes, mushrooms and parsley. Add a cup of hot water—or stock—and simmer until the tomatoes are very soft. Drain the macaroni, pat it dry and turn it into a well-greased oven casserole. Stir in the tomato sauce and the Béchamel—this should be very thin—and plenty of grated Parmesan cheese. Add salt and pepper and bake in a moderate oven for half an hour.

SPAGHETTI
SPAGHETTI

Spaghetti, like rice, is a much-abused food. Properly cooked and served with a nourishing sauce, which has been well flavoured, it is a meal in itself. In Italy, however, it is merely something to start a meal with—an *antipasto*.

In Italy good quality spaghetti is sold everywhere and a good caterer has fresh *pasta* delivered daily. It is possible to buy a fairly good quality spaghetti in Britain and in the cooler weather fresh spaghetti is made in some of the Soho and continental shops.

1 *lb. spaghetti*   *Salt*   10 *pints water*

Bring the water, well salted, to the boil and slowly put the spaghetti into it. Keep the spaghetti in its full lengths. It will become limp as soon as it enters the water and it must swim in it. Cook very rapidly, never once letting the water go off the boil. When the spaghetti is what the Italians describe as '*al dente*'—which means cooked through, but firm enough to be felt when bitten—it is done. The time allowed for cooking depends very much on the quality of the spaghetti. Freshly-made spaghetti takes only ten minutes while other varieties take up to twenty minutes.

When the spaghetti is cooked drain it at once in a colander, and turn it into a serving dish which has been brushed slightly with olive oil and serve as quickly as possible with a sauce and grated Parmesan cheese.

SPAGHETTI WITH ANCHOVIES
SPAGHETTI CON LE ACCIUGHE

1 *lb. cooked spaghetti*   2 *teaspoons tomato paste*
4 *oz. anchovies*   *Chopped parsley*
1 *clove garlic, chopped*   *Grated Parmesan cheese*
1 *tablespoon oil*

Wash and pound the anchovies. Heat the oil, then add the garlic and a large handful of chopped parsley. Brown both, and add the anchovies. Simmer for three minutes, then add the tomato paste diluted with half a cup of boiling water. Stir, and pour the sauce over the cooked spaghetti. Serve with grated Parmesan cheese.

SPAGHETTI WITH FENNEL, SICILIAN STYLE
SPAGHETTI E FINOCCHI ALLA SICILIANA

For this dish you must use the Italian type of fennel which is available in many grocery shops.

1 *lb. cooked spaghetti*	4 *oz. breadcrumbs*
½ *lb. fennel*	1 *oz. pine nuts*
4 *tablespoons olive oil*	1 *oz. raisins*
1 *onion, chopped*	*Black pepper*
1 *lb. fresh sardines*	*Salt*

Fresh sardines in recent years have become available in many parts of Britain. However, failing these, use smelts, sprats or baby pilchards.

Clean and bone the fish. Wash the fennel and boil it in salt water until tender—about twenty minutes. Cut it into small lengths.

Fry the onion in the oil to a golden brown, add the fish and gently fry them, stirring to prevent sticking. Add the fennel, raisins, pepper and pine nuts and then about two cupfuls of tepid water or white fish stock. Continue simmering for another ten minutes.

Pour half the sauce over the cooked spaghetti and sprinkle it with breadcrumbs. Stir well. Serve the spaghetti on individual plates and pour the remaining sauce over it.

Cheese is not added as this is a St Joseph's Day speciality and cheese is not eaten on that day.

SPAGHETTI WITH BUTTER
SPAGHETTI AL BURRO

1 *lb. spaghetti*	3 *oz. grated Parmesan cheese*
4 *oz. butter*	*Salt to taste*

Cook the spaghetti, drain it and place it in individual dishes.

While the spaghetti is cooking heat the butter slowly until it has melted, add salt and pour it immediately over the spaghetti. Sprinkle with grated Parmesan cheese. Garlic lovers should add some pulped garlic to the butter when heating it.

The spaghetti must be piping hot when served this way.

SPAGHETTI WITH MEAT SAUCE
SPAGHETTI CON CARNE

1 *lb. cooked spaghetti*	1 *small turnip, chopped*
¼ *lb. minced beef*	1 *stick celery, chopped*
2 *cloves garlic, chopped*	1 *small parsnip, chopped*
2 *oz. dried and soaked mushrooms*	1 *small tin tomato paste*
	Salt and pepper
1 *sprig each of thyme and parsley*	*Grated Parmesan cheese*
	Butter and oil—about 3 *oz.*
1 *onion, chopped*	*Meat stock*
1 *small carrot, chopped*	

Heat equal parts of butter and oil and sauté the meat for a few minutes, then add the garlic and vegetables and brown them slightly. More than cover them with boiling stock. Stir in the

tomato paste, add salt, pepper, thyme and parsley. Simmer
very gently for two hours. Pass through a sieve and re-heat.
Pour the sauce over the spaghetti. Serve with grated Parmesan
cheese.

SPAGHETTI WITH MARINER'S SAUCE
SPAGHETTI MARINARA

1 *lb. cooked spaghetti*	*Pepper and marjoram*
2 *lb. tomatoes, chopped*	*Bacon rinds*
3 *onions, chopped*	¼ *cup oil*
2 *cloves garlic*	*Grated Parmesan or Romano*
3 *anchovies*	*cheese*
1 *teaspoon sugar*	

Heat the oil and fry the bacon rinds until crisp. Remove rinds
and brown the onions and garlic, then add the tomatoes.
Simmer for five minutes. Remove the garlic and cook slowly
for forty minutes. Stir the tomatoes until very pulpy, add
sugar, pepper, marjoram and anchovies—you will not need
salt. Simmer for another fifteen minutes, then pour the sauce
over the cooked spaghetti and serve with grated cheese.

SPAGHETTI WITH A
TOMATO AND RED PEPPER SAUCE
SPAGHETTI AL' AMATRICIANA

1 *lb. spaghetti*	*handful chopped parsley*
1 *onion*	¼ *cup oil*
1 *lb. tomatoes*	*Salt and pepper*
1 *red sweet pepper*	3 *tablespoons Parmesan or*
1 *clove garlic*	*Pecorino cheese*
½ *lb. cooked minced pork*	

Start cooking the sauce first as it takes longer than the spaghetti. Heat the oil in a pan, brown the garlic, onion and pork. Take out the garlic, add the chopped tomatoes, sliced red pepper and parsley, cook for five minutes before adding sufficient hot water or stock to make a sauce. Add the salt and pepper last. Simmer until the tomatoes are reduced to a pulp, stirring occasionally. The longer you cook the better the flavour, but make sure the sauce does not become too dry.

Cook the spaghetti in the usual way, drain it and mix it well with grated cheese. Pour the sauce over it. Serve extra grated cheese in a deep bowl.

SPAGHETTI WITH SAUSAGE
SPAGHETTI CON SALSICCIA

For this dish you can also use *maccheroni rigati*—a thick ribbed macaroni, nowadays available in Britain.

1 *lb. cooked spaghetti*	1 *glass dry white wine*
1 *small chopped onion*	1 *pint stock*
1 *small tin tomato paste*	*Butter and oil for frying*
1 *lb. Italian pork sausage*	

Slice the sausage into pieces about an inch thick and brown it with the onion in equal parts olive oil and butter. Add the tomato paste diluted with stock. When this has been well blended with the fat, add the white wine. Simmer for at least thirty minutes—longer if possible. Pour the sauce over the prepared spaghetti. No cheese is required.

SPAGHETTI WITH TUNNY FISH
SPAGHETTI CON TONNO

Heat one tablespoonful of olive oil with one tablespoonful of butter. Brown two tablespoonfuls of chopped parsley and six ounces of chopped tinned tunny fish. Stir a little, but try to avoid breaking up the fish too much, add one whole cup of boiling fish stock or water and simmer gently until the sauce thickens.

Add a small glass of white wine, and pour this sauce over about one pound of cooked spaghetti. Serve with grated Parmesan cheese.

VERMICELLI WITH A CLAM SAUCE
VERMICELLI CON VONGOLE

1 *lb. vermicelli*	*Chopped parsley to taste*
2 *lb. clams*	¼ *cup oil*
2 *cloves garlic, chopped*	*Salt and pepper*
2 *lb. chopped tomatoes*	

Fresh clams are not always easy to come by in Britain, but tinned ones are often available and are quite good. If you use them, remember that they are already cooked, so that they only need the last minute heating with the sauce. If you should find yourself in a clam district, choose small clams for preference. They must be well scrubbed and washed in running water until all the sand has disappeared.

Cook them in a steamer for ten minutes—or longer if they have not opened. Strain, save the liquid and take the clams from their shells.

Brown the garlic in oil with the parsley, then add some of the liquid from the clams. Cook for a few minutes, add the tomatoes—chopped and peeled—salt and pepper and cook slowly for forty minutes. Stir the tomatoes, add the clams and cook for just two minutes longer—no more, otherwise the clams will harden.

Cook the vermicelli in boiling water until tender.

VERMICELLI WITH ANCHOVIES
BIGOLI IN SALSA

Heat one tablespoonful each of oil and butter and brown two chopped cloves of garlic. Add eight pounded anchovies and simmer for three minutes. Stir this sauce into one pound of cooked and drained vermicelli.

TUSCANY 'PANCAKES'
CANNELLONI ALLA TOSCANA

1 *lb. noodle pastry* (page 24)   *Ravioli filling* (page 37)

Roll out the pastry very thinly and cut into pieces five inches by six. Drop these into rapidly boiling salted water and cook for eight minutes. Remove them one by one with a perforated slice and lay them flat, separately, on a damp cloth. Spread each piece with stuffing and roll up, like a pancake. Place in a well-buttered casserole and pour over them a sauce—béchamel flavoured with tomato and grated Parmesan cheese is good—and bake in a hot oven until the sauce is a golden brown colour.

RAVIOLI PASTRY
RAVIOLI

Originally ravioli were a speciality of Genoa and even today the Genoese ravioli are considered some of the best. Like so many of these *pasta* recipes they are much simpler to make than one suspects, and naturally there are dozens—probably hundreds—of different ways of filling these little squares of pastry. There are also several recipes for making the dough.

1 *lb. flour*   2 *eggs*   *Salt*

Sift the flour and the salt together, place on a floured board and drop the eggs in the centre. Work the flour and the eggs together, then add enough water to make a pliable but stiff dough. Knead until smooth, then let it stand for half an hour. Cut the dough in half, roll each piece to paper thinness and let it stand for one hour to dry.

Drop teaspoonfuls of any filling you prefer on one sheet of dough, about two inches apart. Cover with another sheet of dough and, with the fingers, gently press around each mound of stuffing. Cut the squares apart with a pastry cutter or very sharp knife and make sure that each ravioli is firmly closed.

Drop into a pan with plenty of rapidly boiling salted water and cook for eight minutes. Remove carefully and serve with tomato sauce and grated Parmesan cheese.

RAVIOLI PASTRY WITH WATER
RAVIOLI

Ravioli pastry can be made—and often is—with water only. While it is obviously not as good as when made with eggs, it is nevertheless quite satisfactory.

Make a firm dough with flour and water, add a pinch of salt and knead vigorously until the pastry is pliable. Divide into two pieces and leave it lying in oil for two hours. You need only a little oil. The pastry should be covered with a cloth during this time and kept warm. When you are satisfied that it is sufficiently pliable, thoroughly wipe all the oil from it, roll it out to paper thinness and leave to dry for two hours before using. Use as for egg ravioli pastry.

FRIED RAVIOLI
PANZAROTTI ALLA NAPOLETANA

Make some very small ravioli—any type of filling will do—and

fry them in deep boiling fat until an amber colour. Serve hot.
Excellent with pre-dinner cocktails.

RAVIOLI FILLING I (VEAL)
RAVIOLI DI CARNE

½ lb. veal
1 small grated onion
2 whole beaten eggs
¼ lb. cooked spinach
½ cup red wine

2 oz. butter
2 oz. grated Parmesan cheese
1 slice bread
Salt and pepper
Stock

Bone the veal. Heat the butter, brown the meat then add
enough stock to cover the bottom of the pan. Simmer for
twenty minutes, add the wine and continue to cook until the
meat is tender. Pass through a mincer, combine with the
spinach, cheese, onion, bread (soaked in milk and squeezed
dry), salt and pepper. Bind with the eggs. Drop in small
spoonfuls on prepared ravioli pastry.

RAVIOLI FILLING II (COTTAGE CHEESE)
RAVIOLI DI RICOTTA

¾ lb. cottage cheese
1 heaped tablespoon chopped
   parsley
3 oz. grated Parmesan cheese

1 egg yolk
1 oz. butter
Salt and pepper

Pound the butter until smooth, then add the egg yolk.
Beat until creamy, then beat in the cottage cheese and the
Parmesan and continue beating until smooth. Add the

chopped parsley and seasoning and drop the mixture in spoonfuls on the prepared ravioli pastry.

RAVIOLI FILLING III (SPINACH)
RAVIOLI DI SPINACI

¼ *lb. cooked spinach*	1 *egg*
Salt and pepper	1 *oz. butter*
2 *oz. Parmesan cheese*	*Nutmeg*

Chop the spinach very finely and, while still hot, beat in the butter. Add grated Parmesan cheese—or grated Romana cheese—seasonings and a good pinch of nutmeg. Bind with a beaten egg and drop in spoonfuls on the prepared ravioli pastry.

SWEET FRIED RAVIOLI
CALCIONETTA

Make a pastry from about eight ounces of well sieved flour, olive oil and white wine. The proportion of oil to wine is one tablespoon of oil to two of wine. Knead it until it is pliable and then wrap it in a cloth and leave it for at least thirty minutes. Divide it into equal halves and roll each half to squares of paper thinness and exactly the same size.

Make a filling from cooked and creamed chestnuts mixed with honey, grated chocolate, grated orange peel and ground almonds. Flavour this mixture with rum and cinnamon and place on the rolled-out pastry as if making savoury ravioli (page 36). Continue as for ravioli but fry the *calcionetta* in deep boiling oil until a golden brown.

Drain them free from surplus fat on absorbent paper, sprinkle with vanilla castor sugar and serve hot.

'LITTLE HATS'
CAPPELLETTI MANTOVANI

Cappelletti are usually served at Christmas and are not cooked in water but in boiling chicken stock. They are made exactly the same way as *tortellini* (page 40) but folded round an elaborate meat filling in the shape of bowler hats. A filling as for *Ravioli di Carne* would be the best, with plenty of pepper (black) and rather highly spiced.

BAKED RAVIOLI
PASTICCIO DI RAVIOLI

24 *savoury ravioli*	1 *chopped onion*
6 *oz. chicken livers, chopped*	1 *chopped carrot*
4 *oz. cooked minced meat*	1 *stick celery chopped*
3 *oz. chopped bacon*	¼ *pint fresh cream*
3 *oz. grated Parmesan cheese*	*Salt and pepper*
3 *oz. chopped mushrooms*	1 *oz. butter*
1 *tablespoon tomato paste*	*Stock*

Cook the ravioli in rapidly boiling water until they are almost '*al dente*' (see page 29).

While the ravioli are cooking prepare the sauce. Heat the butter, then lightly fry the onion, carrot and celery. Add the meat, livers, bacon and mushrooms, and cook slowly for five minutes. Stir in the tomato paste, add salt and pepper and enough hot stock or water to make a fairly liquid sauce. Add the cream at the last moment.

Drain the ravioli and arrange it in a well-greased flat baking casserole. Cover it with the sauce and sprinkle it with Parmesan cheese. Bake for fifteen minutes in a moderate oven.

A second and more simple method is to prepare the ravioli as above, then cover it with a béchamel sauce, faintly coloured with tomato. Add a few very young cooked peas, a little chopped bacon and plenty of grated cheese. Bake for fifteen minutes in a moderate oven.

TORTELLINI

TORTELLINI ALLA BOLOGNESE

These are small envelopes, or half-moons, of ravioli pastry with a filling of mixed meat. The pastry used is precisely the same as for ravioli.

1 *lb. ravioli pastry*	2 *oz. brains, cooked*
4 *oz. pork*	4 *oz. grated Parmesan cheese*
2 *oz. veal*	2 *eggs*
2 *oz. mortadella*	*Salt, pepper and nutmeg*
2 *oz. turkey*	2 *oz. butter*
1 *oz. bacon*	

Mince the meats, bacon, brains, *mortadella* and turkey together. Heat the butter and simmer the minced meats until quite cooked. Add cheese, seasoning and a good pinch of nutmeg. Cool a little, then bind with the eggs—previously well beaten.

Roll out the pastry to paper thinness and cut out rounds the size of the top of a sherry glass. Place a spoonful of the filling on each round and fold over in the shape of a half-moon. Make sure the edges are firmly closed. Cook and serve in exactly the same way as ravioli. The above quantities make about eighty *tortellini*.

BOILED RICE FOR RISOTTOS

RISOTTO IN 'CAGNONI'

It is relatively simple to serve rice that is perfectly cooked with each grain separate yet soft all through. The best rice for risottos and Italian savoury dishes is long grain. Put the rice slowly into plenty of rapidly boiling water flavoured with lemon juice and let it continue to boil quickly for between ten to fifteen minutes. Using a wooden fork, take out a few grains to taste. If they are cooked through, immediately remove the pan from the heat, drain the rice and put it into a well-buttered dish. Dry in a warm—not hot—oven. Stir it occasionally with a wooden fork.

RICE COOKED WITH FISH STOCK
RISOTTO COL BRODO DI PESCE

Heat two ounces of butter or oil in a pan and brown one small chopped onion, a sliced clove of garlic, a stick of celery broken into small pieces, a sliced carrot and two tablespoonfuls of chopped parsley. Add eight ounces of rice, simmer for ten minutes, then add two pints of fish stock. Season with salt and pepper, cover tightly and leave over the lowest possible heat until the liquid is absorbed.

Stir in one ounce of butter before serving and sprinkle with grated cheese.

RICE WITH CRAYFISH
RISOTTO CON SCAMPI

If you buy your crayfish uncooked, first cook them in plenty of cold water to which a cup of white wine, some chopped celery or celery leaves, one carrot and one onion have been added. When the crayfish turn pink, take them from the heat. Peel the fish and pick out the flesh. Put the better pieces aside and rub the rest through a sieve or pound in a mortar. Strain the stock.

Heat two ounces of oil or butter, brown one finely chopped onion, a chopped stick of celery, a pounded clove of garlic and a handful of chopped parsley. Add eight ounces of rice and simmer until the rice looks transparent. Pour over it two pints of strained fish stock and add the pounded crayfish. Stir, then cover tightly and simmer until all the liquid is absorbed. Season with a generous amount of black pepper and flavour with plenty of grated cheese. Remove from the heat. Mix in the rest of the crayfish, or pile this in a heap on top of the rice.

This recipe can be used with lobster, Dublin Bay prawns or shrimps, and can be adapted without difficulty to tinned fish of this type.

If you buy cooked crayfish, remove the flesh from the shells and make a stock by simmering the shells for an hour in water to which wine, chopped celery, a carrot and an onion have been added. Then continue as above.

RICE, MILANESE STYLE
RISOTTO MILANESE

1 lb. rice	Salt and pepper
1 small onion, chopped	2 oz. beef marrow
3 pints boiling white stock	4 oz. butter
½ teaspoon saffron	4 oz. Parmesan cheese

Heat the butter and marrow together in a large saucepan, add the onion and when it starts to brown throw in the rice. Fry until the rice looks transparent, stirring frequently to prevent sticking. Add the stock, salt, pepper and saffron. Mix well, cover and cook over the lowest possible heat until the rice has absorbed all the liquid. Just before serving stir in the cheese and a knob of butter.

NOTE: When simmering the rice in the stock cover the saucepan first with a cloth then with a lid. This ensures the rice will absorb the liquid and be free of starch; and the result will be well separated grains. This is a trick that I learnt in Turkey—not in Italy.

RICE WITH CHICKEN LIVERS
RISOTTO ALLA FINANZIERA

Heat four ounces of butter and very lightly fry one finely chopped onion and as many chicken livers as you require. Add a few chopped mushrooms, half a chopped red pepper, salt, pepper and dribble in one pound of long grain rice. Fry for fifteen minutes, stirring constantly, then add two and a half pints of boiling chicken stock and a quarter of a pint of marsala or sherry. Cover very tightly and leave on the lowest possible flame until all the liquid is absorbed. Serve with grated Parmesan cheese.

MUSHROOMS WITH RICE
RISOTTO CON FUNGHI

Prepared as *Risotto Milanese* (opposite), omitting the saffron and beef marrow and substituting mushrooms. Fry these with the onion before the rice.

TOMATOES WITH RICE
RISOTTO POMIDORO

Cook eight ounces of rice in one pint of stock until tender, stir into it a well-flavoured tomato sauce (page 196) and sprinkle well with Parmesan cheese.

TIMBALE OF RICE
TIMBALLO DI RISO (SARTU)

Sartú, as this timbale is called in Naples, is a name of unknown origin.

First make a plain risotto, using one pound of long grain rice.

Heat one tablespoonful of olive oil, add one finely chopped onion and when this is a pale golden colour add one peeled and chopped tomato, an ounce of dried mushrooms—soaked and well washed—four chicken livers, salt and pepper. Simmer for five minutes then add a quarter of a pint of chicken stock and the same quantity of white wine. Simmer for another fifteen minutes stirring everything well together.

Grease a mould and sprinkle it lightly with fine breadcrumbs. Fill it with the rice, mixed with one tablespoonful of the sauce, two chopped hardboiled eggs and plenty of grated Parmesan cheese. Put it in a very slow oven for one hour then turn it out. It should have a light golden crust. Serve it with some of the sauce as a garnish, and put the rest of the sauce in a sauce-boat.

Similar timbales can be made with brains, calves' livers, sweetbreads, etc. You merely use your culinary imagination and what is around in the kitchen.

SEMOLINA GNOCCHI
GNOCCHI ALLA ROMANA

1 *pint milk*	*Nutmeg, grated*
4 *oz. semolina*	*Butter*
2 *beaten eggs*	*Salt and pepper*

Bring the milk to the boil then add the semolina. Flavour with grated nutmeg, season with salt and pepper and cook slowly for five minutes—or until the semolina thickens—stirring all the time. Remove the semolina from the heat and quickly whip in the eggs. Pour the mixture into a well-greased flat tin and smooth it out to about half an inch in thickness. Leave to get quite cold.

Cut into squares and arrange these in a greased flat casserole. Sprinkle very liberally with cheese and dot with thin slivers of butter. Brown in a hot oven. Grated cheese and a tomato sauce should be served separately with the gnocchi.

POTATO GNOCCHI
GNOCCHI ALLA PIEMONTESE

2 lb. floury potatoes	Grated Parmesan cheese
¾ lb. seasoned flour	Salt

Boil the potatoes until very soft. Drain and pass through a ricer. Mix with the flour and work into a smooth and manageable dough. Roll the dough with the palms of the hands into a strip. Cut into pieces three-quarters of an inch thick and wide. Press your thumb into the middle of each piece and drop, one by one, into boiling salted water and cook for ten minutes. Drain and serve with a tomato sauce and grated Parmesan cheese.

SWEET FRIED SEMOLINA GNOCCHI
LA FRITTURA DOLCE

1 pint milk	Butter
4 oz. semolina	1–2 beaten eggs
2 eggs	Flour
Lemon juice	Breadcrumbs
1 oz. sugar	

Bring the milk to the boil, throw in the semolina and cook it, stirring all the time, until it is very thick. Beat the eggs until frothy, with a few drops of lemon juice and the sugar. Whip this quickly into the semolina. Pour the mixture on to a well-greased board and smooth it out till it is one-third of an inch thick. Leave to cool, then cut into small squares, roll in flour, egg and breadcrumbs and fry quickly in butter. Serve sprinkled with sugar.

An alternative method is to omit the sugar and lemon and serve with grated Parmesan cheese and tomato sauce.

CORNMEAL
POLENTA

This is finely ground Italian wheat corn and used much in Italian cooking. Properly prepared it can be most satisfying.

1 *lb. polenta*   2 *quarts boiling water*   2 *teaspoons salt*

When the water is bubbling add the salt, then gradually the cornmeal, stirring vigorously all the time to prevent it becoming lumpy. Once the cornmeal has been smoothed out and well stirred it can be left to cook for between thirty to forty minutes in an ordinary saucepan, or for one and a half hours in a double boiler. When the *polenta* is ready it should have the consistency of a thick purée and come away from the sides of the pan easily.

Serve in a large flat dish, sprinkle with salt and pepper and pour a rich tomato or mushroom sauce over it. Sprinkle with grated Parmesan cheese.

BAKED CORNMEAL PIE
PASTICCIO DI POLENTA

Prepare the cornmeal as in preceding recipe then pour it into a round greased casserole. Leave it until it has quite set, then turn it out and slice into three layers. Re-grease the casserole, return the bottom layer of *polenta* and spread this with a thick mushroom sauce and sprinkle with grated Parmesan cheese, slivers of butter, salt and cayenne pepper. Cover with the second layer and repeat the mushroom sauce etc, then add the third layer. Brush lightly with butter, sprinkle with grated cheese and bake in a moderate oven for an hour.

Serve with mushroom sauce and grated Parmesan cheese.

If available, make the mushroom sauce with Italian dried mushrooms—they have a strong flavour which goes well with the cornmeal.

SOUP

LE MINESTRE

ALMOND AND RICE SOUP, SICILIAN STYLE

MINESTRA ALLA SICILIANA

2 oz. sweet almonds	2 egg yolks
2½ pints milk	2 oz. butter
5 oz. rice	Salt

Blanch and finely chop the almonds. Cook in half a pint of milk for about fifteen minutes.

In another saucepan bring some water to a rapid boil, add the rice and cook it until it is soft. Then drain off the water, add two pints of boiling milk and bring to the boil once more. Add the almonds and the milk in which they have been cooking, and continue to cook for five minutes. Then pass everything through a sieve.

Return the soup to the pan, add the butter in small pieces and stir it in, add a pinch of salt and remove the pan from the heat. Beat the egg yolks until smooth and then quickly whisk them into the rice mixture. Serve hot.

Sweet soups are popular in various parts of Europe and are eaten like other soups, at the start of a meal.

DR ARNALDI'S SOUP

MINESTRONE ALL'ARNALDI

This soup, which is both nourishing and light, is reputed to have been one of the specialities of the famous Italian dietitian,

Dr Carlo Arnaldi, who would order it for his patients to build up their strength.

Wash about three pounds of mixed green vegetables such as spinach, turnip tops, lettuce and celery tops, and cook them without any more water than that which adheres to their leaves. Add a handful of fresh parsley, one very finely chopped or grated onion and some fresh herbs, salt and pepper.

When the vegetables are soft, chop them and rub them through a sieve. Return to the pan with one pint of hot meat stock, and continue to cook until the liquid is reduced to half a pint. This soup should be thickish but not a cream. Drop an egg into a soup bowl and pour the very hot soup over it. Leave it to settle for a minute or so, then serve. The egg will be sufficiently cooked for eating.

ROMAN BEAN SOUP
ZUPPA DI FAGIOLI ALLA ROMANA

½ lb. red beans	2 cloves garlic, chopped
Stick celery, chopped	1 tablespoon oil
1 carrot, chopped	Rosemary
1 large onion, chopped	4 oz. rice
½ lb. tomatoes, chopped	Salt and pepper
2 tablespoons parsley, chopped	Soda

Soak the beans for twelve hours, then put them into a pan with plenty of water. Add the chopped vegetables, except the tomatoes, and a good pinch of soda and cook until tender—about two and a half hours.

Heat the oil and slowly simmer the garlic, parsley and tomatoes until the latter are soft. Add some chopped rosemary, salt and pepper, and stir this mixture into the beans about half an hour before they are tender. About five minutes before the end of cooking time, take out about one cup of

3

beans. Pass the rest of the soup through a sieve. Return to the pan and bring to the boil, then throw in the rice. Cook for a further fifteen minutes, or until the rice is soft. Just beıore serving return the cup of beans to the soup. Serve in earthenware soup bowls and sprinkle with grated cheese.

Like so many Italian soups this would not be considered a soup in Britain because it is so thick. But it is very nourishing and excellent on a cold night.

The flavour is considerably improved if a piece of salt pork, bacon or even bacon rind is added to the beans. It should be removed before serving.

CHESTNUT SOUP
ZUPPA DI CASTAGNE

1 *lb. chestnuts*	1 *teaspoon salt*
1 *pint milk*	*Pinch nutmeg*
1 *minced onion*	1 *cup cream*
2 *oz. butter*	*Chopped parsley*
Flour	*Pepper*
Handful celery leaves, chopped	

If you have no celery leaves use about a quarter of a teaspoonful of celery salt. If you use celery leaves, chop them very finely.

Slit the chestnuts, roast or boil them until you are able to remove the outer shell and the inner skin with ease. Return them to the pan, and cook them until they are soft. Pass through a fine sieve and mix with the milk. Heat the butter in a deep pan, and very lightly fry the onion until soft, but not brown. Sprinkle with flour and stir. Add the salt, pepper, nutmeg and celery leaves (actually celery salt is easier). When all these ingredients are well blended, gradually add the chestnut and milk mixture, stirring all the while.

Cook slowly for ten minutes, then add the cream. Bring

once more to boiling point and quickly remove from the heat. Garnish with finely chopped parsley and serve very hot with croûtons.

BROTH FROM CHICKENS' FEET
ZUPPA DI ZAMPE DI POLLO

6 *pairs chicken feet*	1 *beaten egg yolk*
2 *sticks celery, chopped*	*Salt and pepper*
1 *carrot, chopped*	1 *tablespoon each butter and oil*
2 *leeks, chopped*	*Bacon rinds*

Continental cooks use parts of the chicken that we are apt to throw away. It should be easy enough to persuade your poulterer to provide you with chickens' feet with which to make this soup.

Wash the feet and singe them long enough to be able to remove the skin and claws with ease.

Heat the butter and oil and brown the bacon rinds together with the vegetables. Add the legs, brown them, then pour in about three pints of boiling water. Flavour with salt and pepper and cook fairly slowly until you have a well-flavoured broth. Strain through a fine sieve, beat in the egg yolk, gently re-heat and serve with croûtons or semolina dumplings (page 44).

BROTH WITH CURD DUMPLINGS
BOMBOLINE DI RICOTTA IN BRODO

6 oz. *cottage cheese*	*Salt and pepper*
2 *eggs*	*Hot broth, about* 3 *pints*
3 oz. *flour*	*Parsley*
Nutmeg	*Olive oil*

Beat the cheese with a wooden spoon until it is creamy, then add the flour, eggs, a pinch of ground nutmeg, salt (not much of this), and pepper. Mix to a firm paste and shape into small dumplings. Leave for half an hour in a cool place.

Roll the dumplings in flour, and fry first until they are golden brown in hot oil, and then drop them into a pan of boiling broth and let them cook rapidly for two minutes. Sprinkle the broth with finely chopped parsley just before serving.

BROTH WITH EGGS
ZUPPA ALLA PAVESE

1 *egg per person*	*Salt and pepper*
Grated cheese	*Chicken broth*
Fried bread	

Place in each soup bowl one slice of bread and sprinkle with cheese. Drop on to each piece of bread one raw egg, taking care not to break the yolk, and sprinkle it with salt and pepper. Pour boiling chicken broth over the egg and almost fill the bowl. By the time you have brought the soup to the table the egg will have set. Serve at once.

BROTH WITH SEMOLINA DUMPLINGS
CHENELLE DI SEMOLINO

2 *oz. semolina*	1 *oz. butter*
2 *eggs*	*Hot broth, about 2 pints*
Salt and pepper	
Pinch of nutmeg	

Soften the butter and then beat it with the eggs until it is creamy. Add the salt, pepper and nutmeg. Gradually stir in the semolina, making quite sure that the mixture is well blended.

Have ready a pan filled with boiling water. Drop the semolina into this in coffee spoonfuls. The semolina will swell and should look like tiny eggs. Cook for two minutes, then drain from the water and drop into a saucepan of hot broth. Cook for two more minutes, then serve the broth with the dumplings.

ONION SOUP
ZUPPA DI CIPOLLA

2 *lb. chopped onions*	*Meat stock*
1 *oz. flour*	1 *tablespoon oil*
2 *oz. grated Parmesan cheese*	*Small croûtons*
Salt and pepper	*Gruyère cheese*

Heat the oil and fry the onions to a golden brown. Mix the flour to a paste with a little milk (or water) and pour this over the onions. Stir and cook for two minutes. Gradually add the stock—about three pints—and continue stirring for two minutes. Cook gently for another thirty minutes, and then pass the mixture through a sieve. Return to the pan, add the Parmesan cheese and about a dozen small cubes of Gruyère cheese. Stir again for a minute or two until all the ingredients are well mixed. Add salt and pepper.

Serve the soup piping hot, preferably in French-type potage bowls, adding croûtons.

EGG AND CHEESE CONSOMME
CONSOMME ALL'UOVO

Break into a bowl as many eggs as you need—i.e., one for each person. Add the juice of a quarter of a lemon to each egg and beat until smooth. Add some hot, but not boiling, stock and gradually thin the egg and lemon mixture. Season with salt and pepper and re-heat very cautiously, taking care to keep the eggs from curdling. Add enough grated cheese to give a good flavour and serve with fried croûtons.

Tinned chicken consommé is excellent for this soup. The number of eggs can be reduced but not too greatly, as this would spoil the soup.

CREAMED ONION SOUP
PASSATO DI CIPOLLA

Stew about one or two pounds of onions in water until they are very soft. Add salt and pepper and then pass them through a sieve. Beat in plenty of grated Parmesan cheese, one egg and a knob of butter. Re-heat and serve hot with fried triangles of bread. This soup should be very thick and white.

MILANESE SOUP
MINESTRONE ALLA MILANESE

8 oz. dried beans	Handful fresh peas
2 potatoes, chopped	4 oz. rice
2 tomatoes, chopped	2 oz. cooking fat
2 courgettes (baby marrows), chopped	1 oz. butter
	1 oz. bacon rinds
2 carrots, chopped	1 clove garlic, chopped
½ small cabbage, chopped	3 oz. grated Parmesan cheese
1 stick celery, chopped	Salt, pepper and a pinch sage
1 onion, chopped	

Soak the beans overnight and cook them next day until they are almost tender. Strain.

Heat the fat and the butter and crisp the bacon rinds. Re-

move the rinds, then add the vegetables and the garlic to the
fat and fry lightly. Pour into the pan about two quarts of
boiling water. Bring slowly to the boil, then add the beans and
cook for ten minutes. Add the rice, salt, pepper and sage and
cook for a further fifteen minutes. Sprinkle the soup with
cheese before serving and stir well.

PARADISE SOUP
MINESTRA PARADISO

2 *egg yolks*	*Salt and pepper*
2 *egg whites*	*Nutmeg*
2 *oz. white breadcrumbs*	1 *oz. butter*
2 *oz. grated Parmesan cheese*	3 *pints hot stock*

Beat the yolks with salt and pepper and a pinch of nutmeg
until very light and frothy. Beat the whites to a meringue
consistency.

Sauté the breadcrumbs in butter until golden. Remove from
the heat and stir in the cheese and the beaten yolks. Stir until
everything is well blended and then add the egg whites and one
ladleful of stock. Mix well, and then pour this mixture into the
rest of the stock, stirring vigorously all the time to prevent the
eggs or the cheese from curdling. Add seasoning and nutmeg,
bring the stock once to the boil and serve the soup immediately.

CREAMED PEA SOUP
CREMA DI PISELLI

3 *lb. fresh peas*	*Grated cheese*
Meat stock about 3 pints	$\frac{1}{2}$ *oz. butter*
Croûtons	

Shell the peas and cook them in the stock until they are soft.

Pass through a sieve. Return to the pan and stir in the butter. Beat until smooth. Serve hot, sprinkled with grated cheese and with very small croûtons. This soup should be almost as thick as a purée.

This recipe can also be used for almost all of the root vegetables, dried beans and peas, and is particularly good for use with chick peas. Always add a really good pinch of soda when soaking dried beans etc.

RICE AND LEMON SOUP
MINESTRINA DI RISO AL LIMONE

6 oz. rice   2 egg yolks
2 oz. Parmesan cheese, grated   Juice of half a lemon
4 pints stock

Bring the stock to the boil, throw in the rice and cook rapidly for twenty minutes. Beat the egg yolks, add the cheese, gradually pour in the lemon juice and stir this mixture into the soup just before serving. Serve at once.

RICE AND PEA-SOUP
RISI E BISI

This soup, even thicker than most Italian soups, was considered by the Venetians as their soup *par excellence*. It was always served by the Doges of Venice at banquets given on the Feast of Saint Mark. I suspect no one was able to eat much after a generous helping of *Risi e Bisi*. As with all traditional dishes, there are several ways to prepare this soup, all arriving at approximately the same result. Here are two recipes.

1.   Fry lightly in butter some bacon rinds, one chopped

carrot, one chopped onion, a stick of chopped celery and about half a pound of shelled green peas. Remove the rinds, add about three pints of hot stock, and then throw in eight ounces of rice. Cook rapidly until the rice is tender, add salt and pepper and serve very hot and thick.

2. Or you can reverse the process. Fry the bacon and chopped vegetables until brown. Add the rice, and when this becomes transparent—about five minutes' frying will be enough—pour in the hot stock. Add the peas and tightly cover the pan. Simmer the rice and peas over the lowest possible heat, and leave until both are soft. Remove the rinds before serving.

This soup one eats with a fork and not a spoon. It should be basically rice, with a green *motif*.

PEASANT SOUP
ZUPPA RUSTICA

1 *cabbage*	8 *oz. broad beans*
3 *leeks*	4 *oz. sliced bacon*
2 *carrots*	6 *small Italian sausages*
1 *large onion*	4 *oz. black sausage (sliced)*
3 *potatoes*	*Salt and pepper*
1 *lb. peas*	*Grated cheese*

Wash and prepare all the vegetables and chop all but the peas and beans into small pieces. Put the vegetables, with the black sausage and the bacon, salt and pepper into a saucepan with about four pints of water. Simmer for two hours. About fifteen minutes before the soup is ready add the small sausages. Serve unstrained with an abundance of grated cheese and croûtons.

The cheese intended for this peasant soup is one which comes from the Lombardy district, but any strongly-flavoured cheese may be used.

POTATO SOUP
ZUPPA DI PATATE

1½ lb. *potatoes, peeled*
1 *onion, finely chopped*
1 *carrot, finely chopped*
1 *stick celery, finely chopped*
2 *cloves garlic, finely chopped*
Handful *parsley, finely chopped*
1 oz. *bacon, finely chopped*

1½ *pints milk*
1 *pint water*
1 *egg*
1 oz. *butter*
2 *tablespoons oil*
Grated Parmesan cheese
Croûtons

Boil the peeled potatoes in two pints mixed milk and water—
one pint of each—until they are soft enough to be mashed
to a cream. Beat in the butter and the egg. Re-heat and stir in
the rest of the milk.

While the potatoes are cooking, fry all the vegetables and
bacon in oil with the garlic and the parsley. Stir this mixture
into the potatoes. When the soup is in the plates, sprinkle with
grated cheese and serve with crisply fried croûtons.

This version of potato soup, like so many other Italian
soups, is very thick—rather like a purée of potatoes—and is
very substantial.

SEMOLINA SOUP
ZUPPA DI SEMOLINO

3 oz. *semolina*
2–3 *eggs*
3 *pints meat stock*

Grated Parmesan cheese
Ground nutmeg
Salt

Beat the eggs until they are smooth, then add the semolina.
You need to make a paste which is neither too firm nor too
runny. Add salt and a good quantity of nutmeg, for this soup
needs plenty of flavouring.

Bring the stock to the boil, then slowly pour it on to the
semolina paste, stirring all the while. Return the thickened
stock to the pan, add three tablespoonfuls of cheese, and cook
for five minutes stirring continually. Serve very hot.

SPINACH SOUP
ZUPPA DI SPINACI

2 lb. spinach	Salt and pepper
Butter	Nutmeg
1 quart stock	Croûtons
2 tablespoons milk	

Wash and thoroughly pick over the spinach. Shake dry and
chop. Melt about one ounce of butter in a saucepan and gently
simmer the spinach until soft. Add salt and pepper and a good
pinch of nutmeg. Gradually pour in the stock and milk, stirring
all the time, and immediately before serving add two tablespoonfuls of croûtons.

A little well flavoured paté or anchovy paste mixed with the
butter gives a slightly different flavour and is an improvement.

CONSOMMÉ STRACCIATELLA
STRACCIATELLA

3 eggs	3 pints consommé or white stock
3 oz. semolina	Nutmeg
3 oz. grated Parmesan cheese	Salt

Break the eggs into a bowl and add the semolina, cheese, nutmeg, salt and one ladle of the liquid. Beat until smooth.

Bring the remaining liquid to the boil, and gradually add

the semolina mixture, whisking briskly all the while to prevent the eggs or cheese from curdling. Simmer very gently for four or five minutes—no longer—stirring all the time.

This is a famous Italian soup, and very simple; yet it is not easy to guess just what makes it so good for its flavour is undefinable.

CONSOMMÉ ZANZARELLE
ZANZARELLE

6 *tablespoons flour*	*Nutmeg*
3 *eggs*	3 *pints stock*
Salt and pepper	*Parmesan cheese*

Beat the eggs and pour into a pan with a lip. Put the pan over a low heat and gradually add the flour. Simmer, stirring all the time, until you have a smooth paste of pouring consistency neither too thin nor too thick. You may have to add just a little milk. Flavour with nutmeg and season with salt and pepper.

Bring the stock to the boil, then immediately lower the heat. Gradually pour in the paste in such a way that it falls like long strings of vermicelli.

The easiest way to do this is to make some very neat holes in the bottom of a clean tin, and pour the paste through this. Stir the stock to give the paste a chance to move around, and when you have exhausted the paste add some grated Parmesan cheese and cook fairly rapidly for five minutes.

GENOESE SOUP WITH BASIL SAUCE
ZUPPA DI PESTO

Prepare a vegetable soup using shredded cabbage, courgettes, green beans, peas, potatoes, tomatoes, etc. Just before it is ready stir into it a basil sauce or *pesto*. There are several recipes for making *pesto*, but probably the following recipe is one of the best. Pound three cloves of garlic together with four tablespoonfuls of finely chopped fresh basil and a little salt. When these ingredients are well crushed, add two tablespoonfuls of grated Parmesan cheese. Mix with just enough good olive oil to make a smooth fairly liquid paste.

CREAMED TOMATO SOUP

ZUPPA CREMA DI POMIDORO

8 *tomatoes*	*Salt, pepper and sugar*
1 *oz. flour*	2 *pints meat stock*
1 *large chopped onion*	½ *cup cream*
1 *tablespoon chopped parsley*	*Butter*

Sauté the onion in butter, then sprinkle in the flour. Stir well and continue cooking for three minutes, but take care that the onion does not brown. Add the tomatoes—peeled and chopped— salt and pepper, a good pinch of sugar and the parsley. Simmer until the tomatoes are very soft. Pour in two pints of hot stock and continue cooking for another fifteen minutes. Rub everything through a sieve, stir in a knob of butter and, if available, half a cupful of fresh cream. Serve with Parmesan fingers (page 16).

TURNIP SOUP

ZUPPA DI RAPE

2 *lb. turnips*	*Sliced stale bread*
3 *oz. bacon ends*	*Grated Parmesan cheese*
2 *oz. butter*	*Salt and pepper*
1 *small onion, chopped*	

Peel and slice the turnips. Heat the butter and fry the chopped onion and the bacon ends. Remove the bacon when crisp. Add the turnips and brown them lightly, and then gradually pour in three pints of boiling water. Add salt and pepper and cook until the turnips are soft. Strain, but reserve the liquid keeping it very hot.

Arrange a layer of turnips at the bottom of a soup tureen and cover with a layer of bread. Repeat these layers until all the turnips are used up. Between each layer sprinkle pepper and grated Parmesan cheese. Pour in the liquid and serve immediately.

The bread should be very thinly sliced and the crusts removed.

Use a light stock if available instead of water—it makes the soup more nourishing and the flavour is better.

CRAYFISH SOUP
ZUPPA DI SCAMPI

24 *live crayfish (Dublin Bay prawns)*	4 *oz. cooked rice*
2 *carrots, chopped*	1 *tablespoon tomato paste*
2 *sticks celery, chopped*	1 *bayleaf*
1 *tablespoon parsley, chopped*	1 *oz. butter*
½ *cup brandy or marsala*	*Salt and pepper*
¼ *pint white wine*	3 *peppercorns*
	Celery leaves

Drop the crayfish into a pan with plenty of boiling water adding one bayleaf, a handful of celery leaves and the peppercorns. After five minutes' cooking, take out the fish and remove the shells. (Pinch with a quick movement the extreme end of the centre fin and take out the intestines and the cyst.) Strain the liquid and reserve it.

Heat the butter in a saucepan and then brown the vegetables

and the crayfish. Dilute the tomato paste with one pint of the fish liquid. Pour this into the pan, then add the white wine and parsley. Cook until the crayfish are very soft. Pour in the brandy or marsala, and continue cooking for a few minutes.

Take the crayfish out of the pan with a perforated spoon and pound them together with the rice in a large mortar. Reduce both to a paste, and stir this back into the soup. Add salt and pepper, stir well and then as quickly as possible pass everything through a sieve. Reheat and serve hot with snippets of fried bread. If too thick add a little more of the crayfish stock.

EEL SOUP
ZUPPA DI CECI

This traditional soup hails from the Lombardy district and is eaten with unfailing regularity on November 2nd, All Souls' Day.

1 *large eel*	2 *carrots, chopped*
1 *oz. butter*	1 *stick celery, chopped*
1 *small onion, chopped*	1 *lb. pig's head or salt pork*
1 *clove garlic, chopped*	6 *slices toast*
1 *tablespoon parsley, chopped*	*Salt and pepper*

Soak the eel in plenty of water for twenty-four hours. Cut it into two-inch lengths. Cut the meat from the pig's head as near the eyes and with as little bone as possible.

Heat the butter in a saucepan and lightly fry the onion, garlic, parsley, carrots and celery. Add enough boiling water to three-quarters fill the pan. Bring to the boil, add the eel and cook this for one hour before adding the meat. Continue cooking for one and a half hours. Add salt and pepper. Remove the meat, take from it any bone and cut it into shreds. Return the meat to the soup and continue cooking until it is re-heated.

Put the toast in the bottom of a soup tureen, pour the soup over it and serve everything as hot as possible.

FISH SOUP

LA BURRIDA

Writers, as well as cooks, have waxed lyrical on the subject of Bouillabaisse, and, while it is generally claimed to have its origin in Marseilles, my Italian friends insist that it belongs just as much to their country, indeed is their Burrida.

It is difficult to make a really genuine Burrida in Britain as the fish required belong properly to more exotic waters than ours. However, a reasonable imitation can be prepared by using gurnet, whiting, haddock, eel, bream, turbot, brill and as many kind of fish as possible.

3 *lb. mixed fish*	1 *bayleaf*
2 *large onions, chopped*	*Saffron*
3 *tomatoes, chopped*	1 *piece orange peel*
1 *head fennel, chopped*	*½ cup oil*
6 *cloves garlic, chopped*	6 *slices fried bread*
Parsley, chopped	1 *oz. butter*

Heat half the oil in a saucepan and lightly brown the onions and garlic. Add the fennel, parsley, bayleaf, orange peel and the tomatoes. Leave to simmer gently while preparing the fish.

Clean and trim the fish and cut into two-inch lengths. Divide the coarse fish from the more delicate. First add the coarser fish to the simmering vegetables, season with salt and pepper and cover with boiling water. Cook on a quick fire for five minutes, then add the rest of the oil, a good pinch of saffron and, lastly, the remainder of the fish. Bring once more to the boil, add the butter, and continue cooking quickly until all the fish is tender. Strain off the fish and arrange on a dish.

Have ready in large soup plates some slices of crisply fried bread. Pour the soup over this. Serve the fish at the same time as the soup. It is usual to eat the soup first, and the fish afterwards, using the same plate. However, there is nothing against eating the soup and the fish together.

The point of the quick boiling is to ensure that the oil and the water blend thoroughly. Take care that the fish is not overcooked, otherwise it will disintegrate. Usually fifteen minutes is enough to cook the fish, but it depends largely on the quality.

Failing fresh fennel use fennel seed.

FISH SOUP WITH NOODLES
BRODO DI PESCE CON TAGLIATELLE

2 lb. fish	Grated Parmesan cheese
1 onion, chopped	1 oz. each butter and oil
1 carrot, chopped	4 oz. noodles
2 sticks celery, chopped	Pepper and salt
3 tomatoes, chopped	

An economical recipe, for you may have fish soup one day and mayonnaise of fish the next. Select firm, white fish—haddock, whiting or fresh cod are perfect.

Clean and trim the fish but leave whole. Heat the oil and butter in a large saucepan, then lightly fry the onion, carrot and celery. Add the tomatoes, lower the heat and simmer until the tomatoes begin to soften. Add salt and pepper, then pour in about four pints of boiling water. Cook gently for another twenty minutes, then add the fish. Continue cooking fairly gently until the fish is tender. Remove it carefully and put aside for later use.

Strain the stock and vegetables through a sieve and return at once to the pan. Bring quickly to the boil, then throw in the noodles. Cook óver a good heat for fifteen minutes, and serve very hot, sprinkled with grated cneese.

If you are not using a fish kettle, it is a good idea to wrap the fish in clean butter muslin and cook it in this so that you can remove it easily. Provided the muslin is washed and absolutely clean it will not affect the flavour.

FISH SOUP, LEGHORN STYLE
CACCIUCCO LIVORNESE

This is a famous Italian dish and considered one of the glories of Mediterranean cooking. An Italian cook preparing it would give full rein to his inventive powers and imagination, and his choice of fish would include octopus, eels (large and small), mullet, *racasse*—a species of fish unobtainable here— and also a kind of waterhen, as well as other fish for which I do not know the English names. However, a passable imitation can be made by using as many different kinds of fish as possible. Each will give to the soup its different flavour. If you do use cuttlefish, wash it under running water and remove the inkbag. Octopus is rather rare in England, and it usually requires some hammering to make it tender. Large eels should be skinned and the backbone taken out, and all the fish should be cleaned and trimmed and cut into small pieces.

3 *lb. mixed fish*	*Wineglass white wine*
1 *whole head celery, chopped*	½ *cup oil*
4 *large onions, chopped*	*Salt and pepper*
1 *lb. tomatoes, chopped*	1 *chilli pepper*
3 *cloves garlic, chopped*	*Boiling water*
Ginger and marjoram to taste	6 *slices very crisp toast*
Lemon juice	

Season all the fish with salt and pepper, and sprinkle it with lemon juice. Heat the oil in a deep pan and fry all the vegetables and one clove of garlic until brown. Add the fish, pour in the wine, and simmer until the wine has almost evaporated. Add boiling water to cover, ginger, marjoram and chilli pepper, and bring once to the boil. Continue cooking over a fairly good heat until all the fish is tender.

Pound the remaining garlic and smear this over the toast. Arrange the toast at the bottom of a soup tureen, cover it with the strained fish, and then pour in the liquid. Serve this soup piping hot and as soon as possible after pouring the liquid into the tureen.

FROGS' LEGS SOUP
ZUPPA DI RANE

In Italy this soup is considered a delicacy, as indeed it should be, for the flavour of frogs is very similar to that of chicken. The hind legs only are used. If not already prepared, these must be cut from the body, washed thoroughly in cold water, and the skin stripped off. It comes off easily, like a glove.

6 pairs frogs' legs
2 tablespoons olive oil
1 small onion, chopped
1 stick celery, chopped
1 carrot, chopped
Handful parsley, chopped
3 tomatoes, chopped
1 clove garlic, chopped
Salt and pepper
3 pints stock (white)
Croûtons

Season the frogs' legs with plenty of black pepper and salt. Heat the oil in a deep pan, fry the onion and the other vegetables (except the tomatoes) and then the legs until they are a golden brown. Add the parsley, garlic and the tomatoes and simmer until these are very soft—about thirty minutes. Pour in the stock, cook for a further thirty minutes, then pass everything through a sieve, pressing the legs well down with a mallet in order to get every ounce of flavour from them into the soup. Return to the pan, re-heat, then serve with the croûtons.

FISH SOUP, TRIESTE STYLE
BRODETTO ALLA TRIESTINA

3 *lb. mixed fish*   1 *tablespoon vinegar*
1 *tablespoon tomato paste*   *Handful of chopped parsley*
1 *clove garlic, chopped*   ½ *cup oil*
1 *large chopped onion*

Cheaper cuts of fish are suitable for this soup.

Clean and bone the fish, then scald it and wipe well with a cloth. Heat the oil in a fire-proof casserole and fry the fish, browning all over. Lower the heat and leave it to cook very gently until it is tender. Take it out of the casserole and put it aside, but keep it warm.

In the same casserole, using the same oil, sauté the onion, garlic and parsley. Add the tomato paste, stir in the vinegar, and then pour in about one pint of boiling water. Cook very slowly for thirty minutes. Return the fish to the pan and simmer until the fish is thoroughly re-heated.

Serve very hot with croûtons.

FISH

I PESCI

BOILED CARP
CARPIONE IN UMIDO

Although carp was at one time popular in this country, it seems to have gone completely out of favour. On the Continent, however, it is still greatly esteemed and often appears at Christmas Eve or on Holy days when meat is not allowed.

Put into a fish kettle or a large saucepan about one and a half pints of red wine—you need enough to cover the fish—a sprig of thyme, two bay leaves, a few thin slices of onion, salt and black pepper. Bring this mixture to the boil, then immediately reduce the heat.

Wash and clean about one and a half pounds of carp, scale it and then put it into the hot wine. Cover and cook very slowly for thirty minutes or until the fish is tender.

In another small saucepan make a white roux and dilute this with warmed red wine. Cook, stirring all the time, for at least five minutes, then pour the sauce into the pan in which the carp is cooking. Stir, until well blended with the rest of the wine, and continue cooking for another five minutes. Remove the thyme and the bayleaves, and then serve the carp with the sauce poured over it and a good squeeze of lemon juice.

STUFFED MACKEREL
SGOMBRO RIPIENO

Carefully clean as many mackerel as you require, make a slit in the tummy of each and remove the centre bone without

69

breaking the fish. It can be done—the art is to rub away at the back of the fish until the bone gradually loosens itself and comes away with comparative ease.

Fry lightly in olive oil some chopped onion, the same quantity of dried and chopped mushrooms—previously soaked—and a good handful of chopped parsley. When the onions are soft mix them with enough white breadcrumbs to give the stuffing body. Add as much grated lemon rind, chopped thyme and grated Parmesan cheese as you like for flavouring. Work all this to a smooth paste and then pack it into the mackerel. Sew up the slits and then, with your fingers, press the fish back into its original shape. It should look as though it had not been touched.

Brush each fish with olive oil, then place them in a well-greased oven casserole. Bake in a moderate oven for about thirty minutes, or until the fish is tender, basting fairly frequently.

Serve with thin slices of lemon and a cold potato salad.

SALT COD CROQUETTES
CROCCHETTE DI BACCALA

1 *lb. salt cod*	*Breadcrumbs and milk*
1 *small onion, chopped*	1 *egg*
2 *tablespoons parsley, chopped*	*Olive oil*
½ *cup thick cheese sauce*	*Black pepper*

Soak the fish for twelve hours in cold water, changing the water two or three times. Wash it well, drain it, and put it into a pan with cold water. Bring to the boil and cook for twenty minutes. Strain, skin and shred the fish and mix with the onion and parsley. Pass everything through a mincer using the coarsest grater.

Beat the egg, stir in the sauce, add plenty of black pepper

and then the minced cod and onions. Leave for thirty minutes in a cool place, then shape into croquettes. Roll in milk and breadcrumbs and fry in deep boiling oil until brown.

Serve hot, sprinkled generously with lemon juice. These cakes make a good breakfast dish and, oddly enough, are excellent with scrambled egg.

SALT COD, VENETIAN STYLE
BACCALA ALLA VENEZIANA

2 *lb. salt cod*	4 *tablespoons olive oil*
4 *large onions, chopped*	*Black pepper*
6 *shredded anchovies*	*Milk*

Soak the cod for twelve hours, changing the water two or three times. Heat the oil in a saucepan, add the onion and brown it lightly. Then add the anchovies, sprinkle with pepper, and last of all add the cod well drained and dried. Fry to a golden brown, then add enough milk to cover and simmer gently until the fish is tender and most of the milk is absorbed. Serve with mashed polenta (cornmeal).

MARINATED EEL
CAPITONE MARINATO

2 *lb. eel*	*Flour*
1 *clove garlic, chopped*	*Olive oil for frying*
3 *cloves*	½ *pint olive oil*
3 *peppercorns*	½ *pint tarragon vinegar*
Salt and pepper	

Skin, bone and clean the eel. Cut it into two-inch lengths.

Wash the pieces and dry them well with a cloth, then roll them in well-seasoned flour. Heat the oil and fry the eel pieces until they are browned. Arrange in a shallow dish and leave until they are cold.

Make a marinade in a saucepan with equal quantities of oil and vinegar. Add the garlic, peppercorns, a very little salt and the cloves. Bring all this to the boil, remove from the heat and leave until quite cold. Pour this over the eel and leave for another twelve hours.

Another method is to clean and wash the eel, dry it thoroughly and roll it in flour, previously well seasoned. Arrange in a large casserole in the shape of a letter 'S'. Cover with the marinade and cook very gently for about forty minutes, basting from time to time. Remove from the heat and leave for twelve hours or even longer. Serve cold.

FRICASSEE OF FROGS' LEGS
RANE IN FRICASSEA

2 lb. frogs' legs	Salt and pepper
1 cup white wine	Milk
4 oz. small mushrooms	Lemon rind
1 pint veal stock	Flour
1 chopped onion	Marsala
1 clove garlic, chopped	Bayleaves, rosemary and
Butter for frying	parsley
Cream	

Usually frogs' legs are sold all ready for cooking. Wipe them with a damp cloth, dip in milk, rub with salt and pepper and lightly dust with flour.

Heat the butter, brown the onion, garlic, mushrooms and frogs' legs. Do not let them become more than a pale golden colour. Add the white wine, simmer for five minutes, add the stock, bayleaves, rosemary, salt, pepper, two strips of lemon rind and cook for ten minutes, by which time the meat will be very tender. Remove the frogs' legs, put them aside and keep hot. Add to the pan a sherry glass of marsala and enough cream to thicken the sauce. Remove bayleaves, rosemary and lemon rind and pour the sauce over the frogs' legs. Serve well sprinkled with parsley, and garnished with triangles of fried bread.

FRIED FROGS' LEGS
RANE FRITTE

Dip the frogs' legs in milk, rub in salt and pepper then coat thoroughly with batter. Dry in deep boiling oil and serve with slices of lemon.

Or—omit the batter—just dust the frogs' legs with flour and dip in beaten egg before frying.

Serve with tomato sauce, or wedges of lemon.

RED MULLET BAKED EN PAPILLOTE
TRIGLIE NELLA 'PAPILLOTE'

Red mullet	*Garlic*
Dried mushrooms	*Oil*
Parsley	*Greaseproof paper or foil*
Bacon	*Salt, lemon and pepper*

The quantity of ingredients for this recipe naturally depends on the number of fish used.

Soak the mushrooms in tepid water for thirty minutes. Wash them well and chop them in small pieces. Chop the bacon, parsley and garlic, and then lightly fry all these ingredients in hot oil.

Clean the fish but do not remove the liver, as this is a delicacy. Cut the paper into heart-shaped pieces. On each piece spread a layer of the mushroom and bacon mixture, then add one fish and spread this with some more of the mixture. Season with salt and black pepper, add a squeeze of lemon juice, then fold the paper firmly round the fish. Bake in a hot oven for about fifteen to twenty minutes. Serve in the paper.

BAKED GREY MULLET
CEFALI AL FORNO

Clean the mullet and score on either side. Rub with salt and pepper. Brush an oven casserole with oil, and sprinkle it well with chopped parsley and lemon juice before putting in the fish. Bake in a very slow oven until tender.

Serve with boiled potatoes—preferably new—tossed in butter and chopped parsley.

RED OR ROCK MULLET,
LEGHORN STYLE
TRIGLIE ALLA LIVORNESE

6 *mullet*	*Thyme*
1 *onion, chopped*	*Bayleaves*
1 *stick celery, chopped*	*Salt and pepper*
2 *lb. tomatoes, chopped*	*Flour*
Parsley	*Oil for frying*

Clean the mullet, season them and roll them in flour. Heat the oil and fry the onion, celery and parsley. When these are brown, add the tomatoes, thyme and bayleaves, and simmer until they are very soft. Pass through a sieve and return to the pan.

In another pan lightly brown the mullet in hot oil, and then transfer them to the tomato sauce. Simmer them gently until they are tender.

Serve the mullet in the sauce, garnished with sprigs of fresh parsley.

If you do not care for fish fried in oil, the mullet can be simply simmered in the sauce without previous browning.

MUSSELS FRIED IN OIL
MUSCOLI FRITTI NELL 'OLIO

Clean, wash and prepare the mussels as in the following recipe to the point of removing the black weed. Drop each mussel into a bowl of good frying batter and then fry in boiling hot olive oil. Drain off the surplus fat on absorbent paper and knock off odd bits of batter—these are apt to adhere and give the flavour of 'all batter and no mussel' unless one is careful.

Sprinkle with lemon juice and serve very hot, either as an appetizer with drinks or in a dish of *fritto misto*.

MUSSELS COOKED IN TOMATO SAUCE, TUSCANY STYLE
MUSCOLI ALLA TOSCANA

4 *pints mussels*	1 *gill water*
1 *onion*	
Thyme and parsley	SAUCE
Salt and pepper	1 *lb. peeled and chopped tomatoes*
1 *gill white wine*	*Oil or butter for frying*

Scrape and brush the mussels and wash them in several waters until all the grit is removed. Put into a large pan the wine, water, onion, thyme, a handful of parsley, salt, pepper and the mussels. Cover and cook rapidly, shaking the pan at frequent intervals. As soon as the mussels open they are cooked. Remove them from the pan with a perforated spoon, take them from their shells and remove the beard. Discard any that do not open.

Heat the butter or oil in a pan, add the tomatoes and simmer until these are soft. Stir to a pulp, add the mussels and simmer gently for two minutes—not a second more or the mussels will harden. Serve the mussels in the tomato sauce with triangles of bread crisply fried and smeared very lightly with crushed garlic.

FRIED OYSTERS
OSTRICHE FRITTE

This is a recipe for which one can well recommend bottled or tinned oysters, or even mussels.

Heat about two dozen oysters in their own liquid, then drain (reserving liquid) and chop very finely.

Put into a small saucepan one gill of fresh cream and the same quantity of oyster liquid. Thicken with flour, stir and cook for three minutes. Add the same quantity of butter as you have of flour and continue simmering gently. Remove from the heat and cool. Beat the yolks of two eggs and whisk swiftly into the sauce. Return to the heat, add the chopped oysters, stir vigorously and cook for one minute. Remove finally from the heat, add six stoned and finely chopped black olives and flavour with salt and pepper. Leave for several hours or until the mixture is very cold. Break off small pieces, form into balls, dip these in a frying batter and then fry in deep boiling fat until brown. Serve with any suitable fish sauce garnished with sprigs of parsley and thin slices of lemon. It is not difficult to prepare oysters in this manner and the result is an interesting and delicious appetizer.

FRIED SCAMPI
SCAMPI FRITTI

Scampi Fritti is a favourite dish of the Venetians, and if you should find yourself within the region of the canals you should certainly order yourself a dish of them. Today in Britain scampi has become the fashionable name for salt-water crustaceans like Dublin Bay prawns (*langoustine*) whether they are true scampi or not. ·

Take the flesh from the shells of as many scampi or prawns as required, dip them in a good frying batter and fry them quickly in a pan of deep boiling oil until they are crisp. Pile on a dish, garnish with parsley and thin slices of lemon, and serve piping hot.

SNAILS, ROMAN STYLE
LUMACHE ALLA ROMANA

Once a year on the Feast of San Giovanni the Romans like to eat snails. With them they drink fairly large quantities of good white wine. The following method of preparing snails is strictly Roman: it takes considerable time, but if you are fond of snails it is probably well worth while.

3 *lb. snails (alive)*	1 *sprig mint*
Vinegar and flour	2 *hot peppers*
8 *anchovies*	¼ *pint oil*
4 *cloves garlic*	*Salt and pepper*
4 *large tomatoes*	4 *slices bread*

Put the snails into a deep pan filled with cold water. Leave for two days, covered so that they cannot escape, but with air to breathe. Throw away the water, then stir into the snails (with your hands) a mixture of salt (*gros sel*), flour and vinegar until

the snails are completely covered with foam. Repeat several
times until there is no more foam. Wash the snails under running water until quite free of the flour and salt, and then put
them into a pan with water to cover and leave them there for
five minutes and drain well.

Fill another pan with cold water, put the snails into this
and cook them over a low heat until they begin to show their
heads. At once increase the heat and cook rapidly for ten
minutes. Strain, and once more drop them into cold water.
Using another pan, heat the oil, add the garlic, the anchovies,
tomatoes, and enough of the snail liquor to make a sauce.
Simmer for fifteen minutes. Add the mint and the peppers and
simmer for another five minutes. Drop in the snails and continue simmering for another forty-five minutes. Remove the
mint.

Serve the snails in their sauce, and leave it to those who eat
them to remove them from their shells. Do not forget to serve
some white Italian wine with them—it is an essential part of the
meal.

MARINATED FRIED SOLE
SOGLIOLA IN 'SAOR'

The Venetians eat this dish on the Feast of the Redemption,.
July 19th.

2 *large soles*	$\frac{1}{2}$ *pint wine vinegar*
3 *onions, chopped*	*Cinnamon*
1 *oz. raisins*	3 *tablespoons olive oil*
1 *oz. flour*	*Salt and pepper*
1 *oz. pine nuts*	

Wash and skin the fish, remove the heads and the fins but do
not fillet. Mix the flour with the seasoning and rub this well
into the fish.

Heat the oil and fry the onions until brown, then remove them from the heat but keep them hot. Put the fish, the nuts and the raisins into the same pan and fry the fish on both sides until it is a deep golden brown. Remove with care and place in a deep dish. Return the onions to the pan, add the vinegar and bring to the boil. Take this sauce from the heat, leave it until cold and then pour it over the fish, completely covering it. Leave it for several hours before serving cold.

GRILLED SWORDFISH
PESCE SPADA ALLA GRATICOLA

Swordfish weighs anything from sixty to three hundred pounds. Its flesh is rather dry but both the texture and the flavour are good. It is a pity that such a fine fish should not often be found in Britain but, as this recipe is typical not only of Italy but of much of the Mediterranean, I feel that it should be included.

1½ *lb. swordfish*	1 *tablespoon chopped parsley*
Juice of 1 *lemon*	*Salt and pepper*
2 *tablespoons olive oil*	

Skin the fish and cut it into cubes about one and a half inches square.

Prepare a marinade by blending the oil and lemon, salt, pepper and parsley, and leave the fish in this for one hour, turning from time to time to ensure that the marinade is well absorbed.

Place the fish under a grill, about four inches from the heat, and cook for five minutes. Remove from the heat, brush with the marinade, and return once more to the grill, this time browning the other side.

If grilling is difficult, roll the marinated fish cubes in beaten

egg and well-seasoned breadcrumbs and fry them in deep
boiling fat until brown.
Serve with slices of lemon and fresh sprigs of parsley.
Halibut may be prepared in the same manner.

WHITEBAIT FRITTERS
FRITTELLE DI BIANCHETTI

These fritters are served with *fritto misto*.
Wash and clean the whitebait and drain on a sieve. Make a
thick frying batter. Drop the fish first into this and then
quickly into a pan of boiling hot oil. Do not put too many in
at the same time otherwise they may stick to each other.
Serve with crisply fried parsley and thick slices of lemon.

TROUT WITH ANCHOVY SAUCE
TROTE IN SALSAD' ACCIUGHE

1 *lb. small trout*	*Salt and flour*
1 *oz. butter*	*Lemon juice and a little grated*
6 *anchovies*	*rind*
1 *tablespoon mixed chopped*	1 *wineglass marsala*
parsley and mint	*Oil for frying*

Empty the trout by the gills, wash them well and dry
thoroughly. Trim, but do not scale. Rub with a little salt and
roll in flour. Fry in very hot olive oil until brown. Arrange the
fish on a serving place but keep them hot.
   In another pan heat the butter, add the anchovies, then the
wine. Stir and simmer for five minutes. Just before removing
from the heat stir in the parsley and the mint—they must both
be very finely chopped—and add a few drops of lemon juice

and half a coffee spoon of grated lemon rind. Pour this sauce over the trout and serve immediately.

When cooking trout in oil, use only the very best grade.

TROUT IN WHITE WINE
TROTE IN BIANCO

2 *lb. small trout*	1 *lemon, rind and juice*
1 *pint white wine*	1 *pint water*
1 *carrot, chopped*	2 *sprigs parsley*
1 *stick celery, chopped*	1 *bayleaf*
1 *onion*	*Salt and pepper*
1 *tablespoon olive oil*	

Prepare the trout as in previous recipe. Heat the oil in a deep pan and lightly brown the trout. Remove them from the pan and put on one side to keep hot. In the same pan brown the vegetables and add the wine, water, lemon juice and the lemon rind cut into strips (but with the pith removed), the parsley, the bayleaf, salt and pepper. Return the trout to the pan and simmer it gently until it is tender.

Remove the trout, arrange on a serving dish and keep it warm while you pass the remaining ingredients (except for bayleaf and lemon rind) through a sieve. Pour some of the sauce over the trout, and serve the rest separately.

If trout is not available, try cooking other small fish in this manner.

GRILLED TUNNY FISH
TONNO ALLA GRATICOLA

Although tunny fish does not often appear on the English fishmongers' marble slabs, it does become available from time to time, and it is worth buying. In Italy it is considered a

4

fish of some delicacy. Its white flesh is not unlike veal in texture and has an excellent flavour.

The best part of the tunny for grilling is the belly cut.
into thick steaks.

Make a marinade with olive oil, thinly sliced onions, one or
two bayleaves, salt and pepper, and a little lemon juice. Leave
the fish in this for about two hours, then grill each steak on
both sides for seven minutes.

Serve very hot with a garlic and anchovy sauce, which it is
advisable to make before cooking the steaks.

ANCHOVY SAUCE: Pound two cloves of garlic with four
or five chopped and filleted anchovies and a handful of
chopped parsley. Add just enough olive oil, drop by drop, to
make a smooth paste. Dilute with a few drops of lemon juice,
and as soon as the steaks are grilled pour the sauce over them
and serve at once.

POACHED WHITING
NASELLO IN UMIDO

1½ lb. small whiting or haddock	2 sprigs parsley, chopped
2 cloves garlic, chopped	Basil
1 onion, chopped	2 tablespoons olive oil
1 carrot, chopped	Salt and pepper
1 stick celery, chopped	1 small tin Italian tomato paste
1 lb. tomatoes, chopped	

Clean the fish and score them two or three times on one side
but leave them whole.

Heat the oil in a large pan; brown the garlic and all the
vegetables except the tomatoes. Add the fish, parsley, basil—
only a little of this—salt and pepper and lastly the tomatoes.
Simmer for fifteen minutes. Dilute the paste with enough fish

stock or water to cover the fish. Pour this into the pan and cook everything gently until the fish is tender. Serve the fish and the vegetables together.

BAKED FISH EN PAPILLOTE

PESCE NELLA 'PAPILLOTE'

This recipe for which you will need greaseproof paper or foil can be used with almost any type of white fish.

6 fillets—not too thick *Butter or oil for frying*
3 oz. mushrooms, chopped *White wine*
1 large onion, chopped *½ pint fish stock*
1 tin crabmeat or the same *Salt and pepper*
*   quantity of fresh crab* *Flour*
1 egg (beaten) *1 lemon*

Almost any type of white fish can be used for this recipe.

Clean the fillets, rub them with salt and pepper and sprinkle them with lemon juice. Heat some butter or oil in a frying pan and fry the fillets until they are a golden brown. Remove from the pan and keep warm. Put the crabmeat into the same pan, stir in the egg, add some salt and pepper and about a sherry glass of wine. Simmer over a low heat stirring all the while, until the egg and wine mixture thickens. Put aside, but keep this warm too.

In another pan fry the onion with the mushrooms, dredge both with flour and stir and cook for two or three minutes. Pour in some white wine to flavour, and then gradually add the fish stock—previously heated.

Cut and grease some squares of cooking paper. Place a fillet of fish on each, spread it with a layer of crabmeat, then cover with another fillet. Pour some sauce over the whole.

Carefully fold up the paper so that nothing can escape and bake in a hot oven for fifteen minutes. Serve in the paper.

WHITING COOKED IN WINE
STUFATO DI NASELLO FRESCO

About 4 small whiting
2 gills white wine
1 onion, chopped
1 carrot, chopped
1 stick celery, chopped

1 sprig parsley, chopped
Salt
Black pepper
1 bayleaf
1 tablespoon oil

Trim and wash the fish and score two or three times on one side only. Rub with salt and black pepper.

Heat the oil in a deep pan, lightly fry the vegetables and the parsley, then pour in the wine. Bring quickly to the boil, add the bayleaf and the fish, then reduce the heat and cook the fish slowly until it is tender—about ten minutes should be enough but it does depend on the size of the whiting.

Take the fish from the pan, arrange on a serving dish and keep warm. Put the wine and the vegetables through a sieve, re-heat and serve this sauce poured over the fish.

FISH STEWED IN VEGETABLE SAUCE
PESCE COL SALSA

2 lb. whiting or small haddock
1 large onion, chopped
1 large carrot, chopped
2 sticks celery, chopped
4 tomatoes, chopped
A little butter and oil
Several bacon rinds

2 cloves garlic, chopped
Basil
Flour
Milk
Salt and pepper
Nutmeg
Grated Parmesan cheese

Clean the fish, remove the heads and tails, but otherwise leave whole. Heat the oil and butter together, fry the bacon rinds until crisp and then remove them, add the garlic, onion, carrot and celery, and when these are browned, the tomatoes. Simmer for twenty minutes or until all the vegetables are soft. Pass through a sieve. Return to the pan, and thicken with enough boiling milk and a little flour to make a sauce in which gently to stew the fish. Add the fish, salt and pepper and a good pinch of nutmeg and chopped basil, and cook until the fish is tender.

Serve the fish in the sauce, sprinkled with grated Parmesan cheese, and accompanied by buttered noodles or plain boiled potatoes.

FISH IN CASSEROLE
PESCE IN CASSERUOLA

2 lb. filleted white fish	1 large sprig parsley, chopped
2 carrots, sliced	2 oz. dried mushrooms, chopped
2 sticks celery, sliced	Fish stock (optional)
1½ lb. tomatoes, sliced	Salt and pepper
1 large onion, sliced	Marjoram
1 oz. almonds	Butter or oil

This is one of the best ways that I know of dealing with those plain uninteresting looking slabs of haddock or cod fillets. If you have no fish stock, then use white wine and water instead. Tinned button mushrooms can take the place of dried when the latter are not available.

Blanch and lightly fry the almonds. Well butter or oil an oven casserole, and cover the bottom with the tomatoes. Add half of the mushrooms, the carrots and celery. Season with plenty of salt and pepper, and pour in enough liquid to cover. Add the fish, then the remaining mushrooms, the onion, parsley and almonds. Bake in a very moderate oven for about thirty minutes or until the fish is tender.

If you prepare this fish casserole in the morning, it is better, for by the time you need it the flavour of the various ingredients has penetrated into the fish. Completely cram the casserole with the fish for it shrinks while cooking and this looks rather ugly when brought to the table.

STUFFED FISH
PESCE FARCITO

1 *large fish*
2 *sprigs chopped parsley*
1 *cup soft breadcrumbs*
Larding or bacon fat
1 *wineglass white wine*

1 *large chopped onion*
Salt and pepper
1 *gill milk*
Olive oil and butter for frying
1 *lemon*

Carp, barbel, large trout, etc. are all suitable for this recipe.

Thoroughly clean and prepare the fish but do not remove the head.

Chop the larding or bacon fat and mix it with the onion, parsley, breadcrumbs, salt, pepper and roe—if any—and when thoroughly mixed moisten with a good squeeze of lemon juice. Lightly fry this mixture in butter then pack it tightly into the fish. Sew up the side of the fish firmly or fix with small skewers, and brush it with olive oil.

Grease a large oven casserole, dredge it with breadcrumbs, and dot the fish with thin slivers of butter. Put it in the casserole, and sprinkle it with breadcrumbs. Pour in the wine and bake for ten minutes in a moderate oven. Add the milk and continue baking until the fish is tender, basting frequently to prevent it drying.

MEAT
LE CARNE

HAM COOKED WITH MARSALA
PROSCIUTTO COTTO AL MARSALA

Naturally the best type of ham to use for this recipe is the Italian raw *prosciutto* with its tangy flavour. Failing this, thin slices of smoked gammon bacon or ham make a good substitute.

Make a roux and dilute it with enough marsala to make a fairly thin sauce in which to cook the ham. Simmer the slices in this sauce for about fifteen minutes. Add a very little salt and pepper.

Tinned sweet cherries with some of their juice, added just before the ham is ready, give the dish that delightful sweet-sour flavour so appreciated by the Italians.

BRAISED BRAINS
CERVELLI D'ABBACHIO IN UMIDO

Blanch the brains for thirty minutes in tepid water and remove the skin and membrane. Put them into a pan filled with water salted and well flavoured with lemon. Simmer for fifteen minutes. Drain and dry the brains, then lightly dust with seasoned flour. Sauté in hot butter, then add one wineglass of white wine and enough hot stock to cover. Flavour with one bayleaf, a sprig of parsley, a clove of garlic, a sliced carrot and a stick of chopped celery. Simmer for thirty minutes.

Take out the brains but keep them warm. Rub the gravy and the vegetables through a sieve to make a sauce. Add to this one well-beaten egg and the juice of half a lemon. Re-heat, whisking briskly to prevent curdling. Pour the sauce over the brains before serving.

Another excellent way to serve braised brains is to cook them as above, then chop them finely and pile them into cooked artichoke bottoms. Mask with sauce, sprinkle with brown breadcrumbs and put for a moment in a hot oven. To be really exotic, pour some brandy in the dish in which they are served and set it alight just before serving. This is a dish for which I recommend tinned artichoke bottoms—they are often available and are very good.

BREADED BRAINS
CERVELLI D'ABBACHIO

Blanch the brains for thirty minutes in tepid water, then remove the skin and membrane. Cook for fifteen minutes in salted water to which a little vinegar or lemon has been added. Drain, dry and cut into thick pieces. Dip in beaten egg and roll in grated Parmesan cheese and breadcrumbs, previously well mixed.

Fry in deep boiling fat until brown.

Serve with a watercress salad or fried parsley well sprinkled with lemon juice.

An alternative method is to sauté the coated brains in butter. Remove from the pan and keep warm. Make a sauce by adding a little red wine to the butter and quickly bring almost to boiling point. Pour this sauce over the brains when serving.

BRAISED BEEF, ITALIAN STYLE
BUE BRACIATO

Lard, and rub with garlic, a good-sized round of beef. Sprinkle it with salt and pepper and flavour it with thyme and rosemary. Heat in a braising pan two tablespoonfuls of olive oil and the same quantity of butter. Brown the meat all over, then add two thickly-sliced onions, two carrots sliced lengthwise and one stick of celery broken into one-inch lengths. Brown the vegetables, add a handful of chopped parsley, one or two thin strips of lemon rind and half a cup of tomato paste previously diluted with one cup of water, and one pint of Italian red wine.

Cook very slowly for about four hours, by which time the sauce will have become thick, and the meat so tender that it almost falls apart at the touch. Slice the meat, strain the vegetables and gravy through a sieve. Pour this over the meat before serving.

SPICED AND BOILED BEEF
RONDELLO DI MANZO

Rub a piece of beef weighing three pounds with garlic, salt and pepper. Make a marinade by bringing one pint of red wine, a teaspoonful of vinegar, one sliced onion, one sliced carrot, a chopped stick of celery, a few peppercorns and three cloves almost to the boil. Leave to cool, then pour this marinade over the beef. Leave for twenty-four hours, turning the meat about three times. Remove the meat from the marinade, dry it thoroughly with a cloth and strain the marinade. Using a braising pan, brown the beef in butter, pour over it the marinade, cover the pan tightly and simmer until the meat is tender, basting occasionally.

ROAST BEEF, ITALIAN STYLE
MANZO ARROSTO

Rub a joint of beef with garlic, salt and pepper, and lard it well.

Place it in a baking tin, with plenty of chopped onion and enough rosemary to flavour. Roast in a moderate oven. Baste occasionally with warm red wine and bake slowly until the meat is tender.

If the meat should be fat, it is not necessary to lard it.

BEEF BRAISED IN WINE
BUE STUFATO AL VINO ROSSO

Rub about two pounds of stewing steak with salt, pepper and grated nutmeg. Place in a bowl, cover with Italian red wine, other red wine will do if this is not at hand, and add two bay leaves and a clove of chopped garlic. Leave for three hours, then dry the meat thoroughly and strain the wine.

Heat some oil in a saucepan and fry three or four bacon rinds, removing them as soon as they are crisp, and brown one chopped onion. Dust the meat with flour, brown, and then add the strained wine marinade. Cover and cook very slowly until the meat is tender. If necessary add either boiling stock or water during cooking if the meat appears to be dry.

BEEF STEWED IN WINE
CARNE IN UMIDO

2 lb. stewing beef	Marjoram or fennel seeds
2 oz. bacon fat or rinds	2 cloves
1 onion	Butter and oil
1 carrot	4 tomatoes peeled and sliced
1 stick celery	White wine
2 cloves garlic, chopped	Flour
Handful chopped parsley	Salt and pepper

Hammer the beef lightly, cut it into cubes and roll in seasoned flour. Clean, peel and chop all vegetables.

Heat the butter and the oil together (about one tablespoonful of each should be enough) then fry the bacon or rinds until crisp. Remove from the pan, and brown the onion, carrot and celery. Add the meat, garlic, cloves, parsley, marjoram or fennel. Cook fairly quickly until the meat is well browned. Add the tomatoes, simmer for five minutes, then pour in the wine, of which there must be enough completely to cover the meat and the vegetables. Cook gently until the meat is tender. Serve either with plain boiled potatoes or rice.

BEEF 'HATS'

CIMA ALLA GENOVESE

1 *lb. thinly sliced steak*	1 *stick celery, chopped*
1 *sweetbread*	1 *onion, chopped*
2 *oz. chopped minced pork*	*Salt and pepper*
2 *oz. breadcrumbs*	*Marjoram*
2 *oz. grated Parmesan cheese*	*Red wine*
1 *lb. cooked green peas*	*Cream or flour*
2 *cloves garlic, chopped*	*Lemon juice*
1 *carrot, chopped*	

Lightly pound the steak, taking care not to tear it. Each slice needs to be large enough to hold one teaspoonful of stuffing, therefore each piece should be roughly two by three inches in size.

STUFFING: Blanch the sweetbread, remove the membrane and skin. Cook in water with lemon juice for fifteen minutes. Remove from the pan and chop as finely as possible. Combine it with the pork, breadcrumbs, cheese, peas, marjoram, salt and pepper to make a stuffing. Moisten with some stock from the sweetbread. Put a teaspoonful of this mixture on to each slice of meat. Fold the meat round the stuffing and mould into hat-like shapes (or balls, if the hats defeat you).

Sew them up with a larding needle or tie with cotton to keep firm. Place the rolls in a pan large enough to take them all flat on the bottom and just cover with boiling water. Add the chopped carrot, onion, celery and garlic and cook very gently until the rolls are tender. Take out the rolls. Rub the vegetables and gravy through a sieve and return to the pan. Add a little red wine to the sauce, thicken with cream or flour. Reheat the rolls in this sauce and serve.

BEEF STEAKS, NEAPOLITAN STYLE
COSTA DI MANZO ALLA PIZZAIOLA

1 *lb. steak fillets*	*Salt and pepper*
1 *lb. sliced onions*	*Oil for frying*
1 *lb. sliced tomatoes*	2 *tablespoonsful cream*
2 *cloves garlic, chopped*	*Flour*
Oregan or marjoram	

Lightly beat each fillet, rub with salt and pepper, dredge with flour and then sauté in hot oil until brown on both sides. Remove them from the pan but keep hot.

In the same oil fry the onions, garlic and tomatoes until brown but not soft. Return the steaks to the pan, add a good sprinkling of either oregan or marjoram and leave the meat to simmer gently in the vegetables until it is tender and has absorbed their flavour.

Stir in the cream and serve the steaks in the sauce.

STEAK, HUNTER'S STYLE
BISTECCA ALLA CACCIATORA

Wipe the required number of beef steaks with a damp cloth

and dip them in well-seasoned flour. Heat some oil and butter together and flavour it with garlic and one finely-chopped onion.

Brown the steaks on both sides then cover them with peeled and sliced tomatoes. Simmer them for five minutes, then add salt, pepper, chopped parsley and a pinch of fennel seed. Continue to cook slowly until the meat is tender. Add a wineglass of marsala or red wine a few minutes before serving.

LAMB, HUNTER'S STYLE
ABBACCHIO ALLA CACCIATORA

Wipe about two pounds of loin or breast of lamb with a damp cloth. Cut into serving portions and rub with salt, pepper and garlic.

Heat in a braising pan enough dripping, or other fat, to brown the meat. Add a sprig of rosemary, a little sage, a whole clove of chopped garlic and one tablespoonful of flour. Stir all these ingredients together then add a cup of white wine and half a cup of wine vinegar. Cook fairly quickly until the sauce is thick, then add a cup of hot stock, cover the pan and simmer the meat until tender. About thirty minutes should be enough. Baste from time to time and add more hot water if necessary to prevent drying. Just before the meat is ready, add four or five anchovies to the sauce.

The meat should be so tender that it is almost falling off the bone, and should be served in the sauce.

If available, add some lamb's kidneys, as they do in Rome.

LAMB MARINATED AND FRIED
ABBACCHIO FRITTO

Wipe a leg of lamb with a damp cloth, rub it with lemon, salt and pepper. Put it into a pan and, using as little water as possible, simmer it very gently until tender. Remove from the pan, leave until cold enough to slice evenly.

Rub a bowl with garlic and lay the slices of lamb in it. Combine an equal quantity of water and tarragon vinegar to make a marinade—enough to cover the meat—adding a little black pepper, two or three cloves, a piece of mace, about an eggcup of olive oil and two bayleaves. Heat the marinade almost to boiling point, allow it to cool, then pour it over the meat. Leave for twenty-four hours.

Dry the meat, dip in beaten egg, roll in breadcrumbs and fry in deep boiling fat. Strain the marinade and thicken it with flour. Simmer a full ten minutes.

Serve the thickened marinade separately. Garnish the meat with slices of lemon and watercress.

PARMESAN CUTLETS
COSTOLETTE ALLA PARMIGIANA

1 *lb. lamb (or veal) cutlets*
2 *eggs*
¼ *cup grated Parmesan cheese*
½ *cup breadcrumbs*

6 *oz. mozzarella cheese*
Salt and pepper
Olive oil for frying

Rub the cutlets with salt and pepper and leave them for half an hour. Beat the eggs. Combine the breadcrumbs and grated Parmesan cheese. Dip the cutlets into the beaten egg, then thoroughly coat them with the mixed cheese and breadcrumbs. Do this twice. Thinly slice the mozzarella.

Heat the olive oil and brown the cutlets lightly on both sides. As each cutlet is ready, place it in a shallow casserole and cover each with a thin slice of mozzarella cheese. Spread with a thin layer of tomato sauce and bake in a moderate oven until the cheese has browned. This takes about fifteen minutes.

Serve very hot with young green peas and potato purée.
Failing mozzarella cheese, use any soft cheese that will slice
thinly and can be cooked.

MILK LAMB CUTLETS IN TOMATO SAUCE
BRACIOLINE D' AGNELLO AL POMIDORO

Milk lamb cutlets are rare in Britain but often lamb or veal
cutlets can be cooked in this way provided that they are very
tender.

Rub lightly with salt and pepper about eight cutlets, then
brown them on both sides in hot butter. Pour over them a
wineglass of white wine and simmer them gently until the wine
has evaporated, then add one wineglass of diluted tomato
paste.

Continue to simmer, very gently indeed, until the cutlets
are tender and have absorbed most of the tomato sauce. Serve
either with chopped spinach, or French beans and slices of
lightly fried tomatoes.

MOCK STEAKS WITH ANCHOVIES
BISTECCHE 'HACHEES'

1½ lb. stewing steak	1 cup red wine
6 pounded anchovies	Sage
2 beaten eggs	Flour or cream
Flour	Pepper
Breadcrumbs	Parsley butter
A little butter and oil	

Put the meat through a mincer and mix it with the anchovies.

Add pepper, but no salt for the anchovies are sufficiently salty, and bind with one egg. Knead and shape into steaks. Roll them in flour, the remaining egg, and very fine breadcrumbs.

Heat the oil and butter together, add the sage (fresh if available) and lightly brown the steaks on both sides. Pour in the wine fairly slowly and continue cooking until it has evaporated. Add a little boiling water and simmer until the 'steaks' are quite cooked through, turning them over once during cooking.

Remove from the pan and place on each 'steak' a pat of parsley butter and one or two thin strips of anchovy. Thicken the gravy with either a little flour or cream and serve separately.

MEAT BALLS, FLORENTINE STYLE
POLPETTINE ALLA FIORENTINA

10 oz. minced beef	1 stick celery, chopped
2 oz. minced bacon	1 carrot, chopped
2 oz. grated cheese	Salt, pepper, nutmeg
1 beaten egg	Stock
3 tablespoonsful brown bread-	Butter or oil for frying
crumbs	Flour
1 onion, chopped	

Mince the meat, bacon and onion together twice. Heat a little butter or oil, fry the meat for five minutes then add two or three ladles of stock and simmer gently until the meat is cooked through. Remove it from the stove and when it is cool add the egg, breadcrumbs, cheese, salt, pepper and nutmeg. Mix everything to a paste, then shape it into balls. Roll in flour.

Heat a little more butter or oil, brown the celery and carrot and then the meat balls. Pour in enough stock to almost cover and simmer gently for thirty minutes. Take the balls from the pan with a perforated spoon and keep them warm in a serving dish. Put the vegetables and stock through a sieve, and pour this gravy over the meat balls.

MEAT BALLS ON SKEWERS
SPIEDINI

1 *lb. minced raw beef*	1 *clove garlic, chopped*
2 *beaten eggs*	*Salt and pepper*
2 *oz. grated cheese*	*Bacon cut into squares*
4 *oz. breadcrumbs*	*Bread cut into cubes*
2 *tablespoons chopped parsley*	*Oil for frying*

Combine the meat, parsley, cheese, breadcrumbs, garlic, salt and pepper and pass once through a mincer. Bind with the eggs. Shape into 'bullets' and leave for half an hour either in a refrigerator or other very cold place.

Thread the *spiedini* on to skewers with a cube of bread and a piece of bacon between each *spiedini*. Fry in deep boiling oil and serve on the skewers with a plain rice risotto.

The *spiedini* can also be grilled. Brush them with olive oil and place at least four inches below the heat. Grill for about fifteen minutes, turning several times.

ROAST LAMB IN ANCHOVY SAUCE
ABBACCHIO IN SALSA D'ACCIUGHE

Wipe a leg of lamb with a damp cloth. Make several gashes in the flesh with a sharp knife and insert into these slivers of garlic. Rub the meat with salt, pepper and a little ground ginger. Place on the trivet in a roasting pan and bake in a moderate oven until tender. Baste first with a warmed white wine, then with hot stock or water.

Remove the meat, and mix with the gravy three or four

anchovies, a handful of finely chopped parsley and a teaspoonful of grated lemon rind.

Stir all these ingredients together, bring to the boil, thicken slightly with flour, cook for five minutes, then serve meat and sauce separately.

ROASTED SUCKING LAMB
AGNELLINO AL FORNO

Both young lamb and kid are prepared as an Easter speciality in Italy. Occasionally in London's Italian shops one is able to buy a whole kid, and of course a lamb. The same recipe, however, does for both. Kid, when properly prepared, is very good.

1 *lamb—about 7 to 8 lb.*	*Salt, pepper and ginger*
1 *lb. cooking apples*	*Larding or bacon rashers*
6 *sliced cloves garlic*	*Lemon juice and peel*
Cloves	*Oil or butter*
Cream or flour	

Rub the prepared lamb (or kid) inside and out with lemon juice and peel. Core the apples, wrap them in strips of larding, or fat bacon, and push a clove into each. Stuff these into the lamb and sew it up neatly. With a sharp knife make slits on either side of the lamb and insert slivers of garlic. Rub it with a mixture of salt, pepper and ginger, and brush with hot oil or butter.

Roast until tender in a moderate oven, allowing about fifteen minutes to the pound, and basting every fifteen minutes with boiling water or hot apple juice. Remove from the pan and thicken the gravy with cream or flour and pass it through a sieve.

FRIED LIVER
FEGATO FRITTO ALLA SALVIA

Thinly slice the liver and leave it to soak for one hour in milk. Drain, dry thoroughly, then roll it in flour flavoured with pepper.

Heat a little butter and flavour it with sage. Very slowly fry the liver until tender, shaking the pan from time to time to prevent burning.

Remove the liver. Add enough flour to the butter to make a roux, then thin to a sauce with red wine. Stir the sauce well, strain and pour over the liver before serving.

BRAISED LIVER, TRIESTE STYLE
FEGATO ALLA TRIESTINA

1 *lb. liver*	1 *clove garlic*
1 *tablespoon breadcrumbs*	*Handful parsley*
1 *onion* ⎫	*Pepper, sage and cloves*
1 *carrot* ⎬ *chopped*	*Lemon*
1 *stick celery* ⎭	½ *cup oil for frying*
½ *lb. sliced tomatoes*	*Fried bread*

Scald the liver for five minutes in boiling water. Drain it, and cut it into slices. Stick one clove into each slice. Heat the oil, and fry the breadcrumbs, onion, carrot and celery until a light brown.

Arrange the liver on top of the vegetables. Add the tomatoes, pepper, sage and garlic and just cover with cold water. Cover, bring once to the boil, then simmer until the liver is tender. Remove the liver from the pan, remove cloves, and arrange it in the middle of a serving dish surrounded by fingers of crisply fried bread.

Rub the gravy and vegetables through a sieve and pour this over the bread. Add a good squeeze of lemon and garnish with parsley.

LIVER AND ONIONS
FEGATO ALLA VENEZIANA

¾ *lb. calves' liver*	*Flour*
2 *large onions, chopped*	*Paprika pepper*
1 *tablespoon parsley*	*Black pepper*
1 *wineglass red wine*	1 *oz. each butter and oil*

This simple dish is claimed by the Venetians as their invention, and it has, whatever its origin, become a national and international dish.

Wash the liver in cold water, dry it thoroughly and slice it thinly. Roll it in flour seasoned with black and with paprika pepper.

Heat the butter and oil together and brown the onions. Add the liver, lightly brown it on both sides, then add the wine. Simmer for five minutes, add the parsley and continue to simmer gently until the liver is tender.

PORK CUTLETS
MARINATED AND GRILLED
COSTOLETTE DI MAIALE MARINATE

Rub a mixing-bowl with garlic and make a marinade with about a quarter of a pint of tarragon vinegar, the same quantity of white wine and two tablespoonfuls of olive oil. Flavour with salt, chopped parsley, a clove, nutmeg, a small onion and black pepper. Whip up well and leave the cutlets in it for two hours.

Take the cutlets from the marinade and grill them on both sides until tender. Serve with a hot caper sauce.

MORTADELLA FRITTERS
COTOLETTE DI MORTADELLA

Dip as many thick slices of mortadella as required in a thick coating of batter to which some béchamel sauce has been added. Fry in deep boiling fat until a golden brown.

TIPSY PORK
MAIALE UBRIACO

Rub as many pork chops as required with lemon, salt and pepper. Grease a pan and heat it well before adding the chops. Brown on both sides over a low heat, then add red chianti or other red wine to cover. Simmer gently until the chops are tender, turning them at least once. Much of the wine will have been absorbed during the cooking, but what is left should be poured over the chops when serving.

ROAST PORK WITH PRUNE SAUCE
LOMBATINE DI MAIALE CON SALSA DI PRUGNE

Score a roast of pork and rub with lemon juice, garlic, salt and pepper. Put it into a roasting pan, with a little rosemary, the juice of one lemon and a cup of boiling water. Roast in a moderate oven, basting fairly often. Just before the pork is ready baste it with a quarter of a pint of white wine and continue to bake until the wine has evaporated. Serve with a prune sauce (page 194).

BRAISED OX-TONGUE
LINGUA DI BUE BRACIATA

1 *tongue*	*½ pint white wine*
6 *anchovies*	1 *tablespoon cream*
1 *tablespoon capers*	*Larding*
1 *clove garlic, chopped*	*Bacon rinds*
1 *carrot, chopped*	*Salt and pepper*
1 *gherkin, chopped*	*A little oil and butter*
Parsley and basil	

Soak the tongue for one hour in salted water. Drain and trim
it, then boil it rapidly until you can remove the skin with ease.
Lard it and put pieces of anchovy in between the larding.

Heat the oil with the butter and fry the bacon rinds until
crisp. Remove bacon rinds, brown the carrot, garlic, parsley—
a good handful of this—and basil. Add the tongue, brown it,
then pour in the wine. Simmer for a few minutes then add
enough boiling water to cover. Add salt and pepper and one
more tablespoonful of oil. Simmer gently for about four hours,
or until the tongue is tender.

Remove the tongue from the pan, and keep it warm. Rub the
gravy and the vegetables through a sieve. Return to the pan,
add the gherkin, the capers and a tablespoonful of cream.
Simmer and stir to a smooth sauce. Serve the tongue together
with the sauce.

TONGUE WITH A SOUR-SWEET SAUCE
LINGUA DI BUE IN SALSA AGRODOLCE

Make a white roux, add salt and pepper and enough red wine
and stock to make a sauce. Add two tablespoonsful of brown
sugar, one tablespoonful of pine nuts and one of raisins and a

heaped tablespoonful of grated orange peel. Simmer these ingredients for about fifteen minutes. Add as much sliced cooked tongue as required, pour in a glass of sherry and continue to cook gently for another ten minutes.

Serve the tongue in the sauce and garnish with watercress.

TRIPE, MILAN STYLE
BUSECCA (TRIPPA ALLA MILANESE)

3 lb. tripe	½ lb. fresh broad beans
2 onions	3 tablespoons tomato paste
3 leeks	Grated Parmesan cheese
4 tomatoes	4 bacon rinds
2 sticks celery	Saffron and nutmeg
2 carrots	Salt and pepper
1 lb. potatoes	Butter and oil
½ small cabbage	3 cloves
Parsley	Slices of bread

Wash and scrape the tripe. Cut into serving pieces, cover with cold water, bring to the boil and cook for five minutes. Drain, throw away the water, cover once more, this time with boiling water. Add one stick of celery and one onion stuck with cloves. Bring to the boil and continue to cook over a moderate heat for two hours. Take out the tripe, thoroughly dry it, then if desired, marinate it in a vinegar and oil dressing for several hours. Strain the stock and reserve for later use.

Clean and slice or chop remaining vegetables. Fry the bacon rinds in equal parts of oil and butter, then brown the beans, carrots, leeks, the remaining onion and the celery. Add the tomatoes, simmer for fifteen minutes, then add the tripe, salt, pepper, saffron and nutmeg. Simmer for a further five minutes, add the strained stock, potatoes, cabbage, tomato paste and parsley. Continue to cook slowly until everything is tender.

Then stir in plenty of grated Parmesan cheese. Serve in a tureen with fingers of bread, rubbed with garlic and fried in oil, floating on top.

RAGOUT OF VEAL

OSSOBUCO

This is one of the great dishes of Milan and is always served with rice, usually *risotto milanese*. There are two main points in the preparation ot this dish, its flavouring, the *gremolata*, and the precious marrow from the bones. In most Italian homes and restaurants a small marrow fork is offered with which to dig out this delicacy which is usually spread on chunks of bread.

6 *veal shin bones or veal shanks*	4 *oz. butter*
6 *large tomatoes*	1 *cup of wine*
Salt and pepper	1 *clove garlic, minced*
Flour	1 *teaspoon grated lemon rind*
	2 *tablespoons minced parsley*

The bones should each be between two and a half to three inches long and with some meat attached. Many butchers will correctly chop the bones for this dish if asked. Peel, seed and chop the tomatoes. Sprinkle the bones with salt, pepper and dredge lightly with flour. Heat the butter in a large saucepan, add the bones and brown them all over. Stand the bones in the pan so that they are upright and the marrow cannot fall out. Add the wine, cook for ten minutes, then add the tomatoes. Cover the pan tightly and simmer until the meat on the bones is so tender it almost falls off. About one to one and a half hours.

Mix the remaining ingredients to make the *gremolata* and sprinkle over the bones three minutes before serving.

To present *ossobuco* in the classical fashion, serve it surrounded by the risotto and with a dressing of melted butter and grated Parmesan cheese.

VEAL 'BIRDS'
VITELLO ALL'UCCELLETTO

Only the very tenderest of veal fillets are suitable for this.

Heat a little butter and oil together, add garlic and one bay-leaf. As this begins to brown, fry the fillets on both sides, sprinkling them with salt and pepper as they cook. As soon as they are browned, place them on a serving plate. Remove the garlic and bayleaf from the pan and pour the fat drop by drop on to the meat. Serve at once.

The flavour and virtue of this dish depends entirely on the quality of the veal and the accompanying ingredients, i.e., the butter and oil—and the speed with which the veal appears on the table after it has been cooked.

Another way to prepare veal 'birds' is to cut the fillets into cubes and push these on to a skewer with a piece of bacon between each cube. Sprinkle with salt, pepper and chopped rosemary, then grill under a good heat. They need no other accompaniment than the fat and meat juice which falls into the grill pan.

VEAL ROLLS A LA ROSSINI
INVOLTINI DI VITELLO ALLA ROSSINI

1 *lb. veal*	1 *small onion, sliced*
3 *oz. chopped bacon*	*Butter for frying*
1 *tablespoon chopped parsley*	*Sage or rosemary*
3 *slices white bread*	*Several cubes white bread*
3 *oz. grated Parmesan cheese*	*Oil for frying*
1 *clove garlic, sliced*	*Salt and pepper*
Lemon juice	*Beaten egg and breadcrumbs*

Slice the veal thinly, then cut into three-inch squares. Lightly pound until the squares are very thin but try to keep their shape.

Soak the slices of bread in milk and squeeze them dry. Lightly fry the bacon in butter adding the onion and garlic. Combine with the soaked bread, cheese, parsley, salt and pepper. Knead to a paste and place a teaspoonful of the mixture in the middle of each slice of veal. Roll firmly and secure each roll either with cotton or with toothpicks.

Dip each roll in lemon juice, beaten egg and breadcrumbs. Fix on long skewers, alternating with cubes of bread. Sprinkle with chopped sage or rosemary and fry in deep hot oil until browned all over.

Serve very hot on the skewers.

Another method is to ignore the stuffing and spread each veal slice with anchovy paste and crushed capers.

VEAL WITH TUNNY FISH AND ANCHOVIES
VITELLO TONNATO

2 lb. lean veal	3 cloves
8 anchovies	Juice of one lemon
5 oz. tinned tunny fish	White wine
2 egg yolks	Olive oil
1 carrot, chopped	Capers
1 stick celery, chopped	Salt and pepper
2 bayleaves	

Soak the veal for half an hour in cold water, dry it well and put it into a saucepan with a very small quantity of water. Add the vegetables, lemon juice, cloves, bayleaves, salt and pepper and half a glass of white wine. Bring once to the boil then cook slowly until the veal is tender. Remove the meat, leave it to cool

and continue to cook the liquid until it is reduced by half.
Strain.

Pound the tunny fish in a mortar with the anchovies, then
rub both through a very fine sieve. Beat the egg yolks with a
wooden spoon, add to them—drop by drop—enough olive oil
to make a fairly fluid dressing. Blend in the veal gravy, add the
pounded fish and whisk until the dressing is smooth. Lastly
add a few chopped capers.

Slice the meat, spread each slice with the dressing and
arrange in a casserole. Cover and leave for several hours in a
cool place before serving.

Garnish with thin slices of lemon and fresh parsley.

VEAL FILLETS WITH HAM
SALTIMBOCCA

A recipe which, while it finds its origin in Brescia, is so popular in Rome that it has become a Roman speciality. For four
people you need eight thin slices of veal and the same amount
of ham. Lightly hammer the veal, rub with lemon, salt and
pepper and on each slice put a leaf of fresh sage. Cover with a
slice of ham or thin bacon. Fix with a toothpick and fry
in oil or butter as quickly as possible.

Serve with artichokes, young peas, tiny brussels sprouts or
new potatoes.

LIVER, TUSCAN STYLE
FEGATO ALLA TOSCANA

This is simply calves' liver, sliced horizontally, seasoned with
black pepper, flavoured with sage, and fried in deep hot oil.

VEAL FILLETS WITH EGG SAUCE
BISTECCHINE DI VITELLO ALLO ZABAIONE

This is rather extravagant, a little exotic, but very good.

6 *veal fillets*	2 *beaten egg yolks*
6 *slices bread*	1 *wineglass marsola*
Salt, pepper, sugar	*Butter for frying*
Lemon juice	

First make the sauce. Season the eggs and add just one table-spoonful of sugar, then whip in the wine and one tablespoonful of boiling water. Put this mixture into the top of a double-boiler and cook it slowly, stirring all the time, until it is thick. Put aside, but keep it warm.

Trim the veal fillets until each is exactly the same shape and size. Very lightly hammer each and rub with lemon juice, salt and pepper. Sauté in butter, browning on both sides. Fry the bread—each slice should be the same shape but a little larger than the veal fillets.

Put one veal fillet on each slice of bread, cover with the egg sauce (*zabaione*) and serve immediately.

VEAL WITH MARSALA
SCALOPPINE AL MARSALA

Flatten as many veal fillets as required and rub with lemon juice. Dust with seasoned flour and brown quickly on both sides in butter. Add a good glassful of marsala and continue to cook very slowly until the meat is tender.

Serve garnished with fresh watercress and slices of lemon.

POULTRY AND GAME
I POLLI

CHICKEN ARETINA
POLLO ALL'ARETINA

2 *plump dressed chickens*	*Olive oil for frying*
2 *chopped onions*	½ *lb. shelled garden peas*
2 *wineglasses white wine*	4 *oz. rice*
1 *pint stock*	*Salt and pepper*

Joint the cleaned chickens into suitable serving pieces, and rub each with salt and pepper. Heat the olive oil in a pan, lightly fry the onions, and just as these begin to change colour add the chicken pieces. Brown these well, pour in the wine, simmer for five minutes, then add the stock. Bring once to the boil, add the rice and the peas, salt and pepper. Cook over a moderate heat for twenty minutes.

Serve everything together.

CHICKEN BAKED IN CREAM
POLLO ALLA CREMA

Joint a plump and dressed small chicken into serving pieces. Lightly rub with lemon and then roll in seasoned flour. Heat a fairly large piece of butter in an oven casserole and brown the chicken pieces on top of the stove. Pour in enough fresh cream to cover the chicken completely, and then put the casserole into a moderate oven and bake the chicken until tender, basting from time to time with the cream.

Remove the chicken from the casserole and keep warm. Thicken the cream with the thinnest possible potato flour and water paste, add one more cup of cream, a good flavouring of brandy and bring all just to the point of boiling. Serve the chicken in the sauce.

One way to serve chicken cooked in cream is to make a rice ring and to serve the chicken in the centre with the sauce poured over it. This is a delicious dish but cannot be made with substitutes—it's butter and cream or nothing.

CHICKEN MARSALA
POLLO MARSALA

Joint a dressed chicken, rub it well in seasoned flour, then brown it either in olive oil or butter. Add enough marsala to cover, and simmer gently until tender. Serve in the sauce.

CHICKEN MADDALENA
POLLO ALLA MADDALENA

1 *chicken*	*Boiling stock*
1 *sliced onion*	1 *dozen black olives*
2 *cloves garlic, sliced*	4 *anchovies*
1 *tablespoon chopped parsley*	1 *bayleaf*
1 *stick chopped celery*	½ *cup olive oil for frying*
1 *wineglass brandy*	*Salt and pepper*

Joint a dressed chicken into serving pieces. Rub with salt, pepper and the bayleaf.

Heat the oil and fry the onion, celery, garlic and parsley to a light brown. Add the chicken pieces and fry these until golden. Pour in the brandy, simmer until this has evaporated and then add enough boiling stock to cover. Continue to cook slowly until the chicken is tender, then add the olives—stoned and chopped—and just before serving, the anchovies.

This is simple and good and does a good deal to the flavour
of a battery-fed bird.

CHICKEN, HUNTER'S STYLE
POLLO ALLA CACCIATORA

1 *or* 2 *chickens*	2 *tablespoons chopped parsley*
1 *large chopped onion*	1 *rasher diced bacon*
2 *cloves garlic*	*Salt and pepper*
4 *tomatoes peeled and sliced*	*Hot stock*
2 *wineglasses white wine*	½ *cup olive oil*

Joint the chickens and rub them with salt and pepper. Heat the
oil, lightly fry the onion, add the chicken pieces, and when
these are a golden brown, add the garlic and the wine and
simmer for about ten minutes. Add the tomatoes, bacon and
parsley, simmer for another ten minutes or so, remove the
garlic, and then almost cover the chicken with boiling stock.
Cook slowly until the chicken is tender.

CHICKEN, NEAPOLITAN STYLE
POLLO ALLA NAPOLETANA

1 *boiling fowl*	1 *oz. Italian bacon or ham*
4 *oz. dried mushrooms*	2 *wineglasses white wine*
2 *cloves garlic, sliced*	*Rosemary*
2 *tablespoons tomato paste*	2 *oz. each oil and butter*
2 *large onions, chopped*	*Salt and pepper*

Rub the bird with salt and pepper, put it into a pan with
plenty of salted water, cover well and cook slowly until it is
tender—about two to three hours, depending on the age of the
bird.

The mushrooms may be chopped or left whole; soak them
for half an hour in tepid water. Dice the bacon.

Heat the oil and butter together in a pan and fry the onions until they begin to change colour, then add the mushrooms, bacon, garlic and rosemary. Simmer gently until the onions are soft, stir in the tomato paste and two tablespoonfuls of the chicken stock. Continue to simmer for another ten minutes, then add the wine.

Take the chicken from the pan and joint it. Place the pieces in the sauce and leave them to simmer until they have absorbed some of its flavour. Serve the chicken in the sauce.

This is an excellent way to deal with tough birds—the sauce gives it flavour and from the boiling you have a pot of stock for making soup.

CHICKEN SPATCHCOCK
POLLO ALLA DIAVOLA

This very simple but usually successful method of grilling chickens belongs to Tuscany, and the chicken is eaten traditionally at the Feast of the Impruneta, accompanied by a bottle or two of good Chianti wine. It needs very young and plump chickens, and without these there is no point in attempting it.

Split open from the back as many young chickens as required. Spread out and flatten—use a heavy iron—and rub with lemon juice. Fix them with skewers to keep them flat and lay them in a marinade of olive oil, chopped parsley, onion, ground ginger and plenty of salt and pepper. Leave them there for several hours, for one of the secrets of this dish is the subtle flavour of ginger. Place the chickens under a hot grill and brown on both sides. Remove the skewers, garnish the chickens with slices of lemon, and serve with a fresh watercress salad.

I need hardly say that the flavour of these chickens is even better when they are grilled over a charcoal fire.

Pigeons, provided that they are tender, may be prepared in the same way.

Serve with a sauce.

CHICKEN, ROMAN STYLE
POLLO ALLA ROMANA

1 dressed chicken	Rosemary
1 wineglass white wine	2 rashers bacon
1 clove garlic, sliced	½ cup oil
1 small tin tomato paste	Stock, salt and pepper

Joint the chicken, rub the pieces with salt and pepper and then brush with olive oil. Dice the bacon. Heat the oil in a deep pan, add the bacon, the garlic and then the chicken pieces, and fry until they are a golden brown. Sprinkle them with chopped rosemary, salt and pepper, pour in the wine and simmer for several minutes. Add the tomato paste and enough hot stock to make a sauce. Cook slowly until the chicken pieces are tender, and serve in the sauce.

CHICKEN STEW
POLLO IN UMIDO

1 large boiling fowl	2 oz. dried mushrooms
2 large onions, chopped	1 dozen green olives
2 green peppers, chopped	1 cup oil
6 peeled tomatoes, chopped	Flour for thickening
1 teaspoon sugar	Salt and pepper
1 lb. shelled garden peas	

Joint the fowl into serving portions. Rub the pieces with salt and pepper and then with flour. Heat the oil and brown the

5

chicken pieces. Remove them and keep them hot. In the same oil fry the onions, peppers, olives and tomatoes for about fifteen minutes. Add the sugar then replace the chicken pieces and pour in sufficient hot water to cover. Cook slowly, tightly covered, until the chicken pieces are almost tender. Add the peas, the mushrooms—previously soaked and chopped —and a thin flour and water paste. Cover the pan again and continue to cook gently until the peas are soft.

You can also add rice to this stew at the same time as you add the peas. A good pinch of saffron adds a different and distinctive flavour, but this should not be added until the chicken has been cooking for about one hour.

BRAISED DUCK WITH LENTILS
ANITRA CON LENTICCHIE

1 *duck*	½ *cup olive oil*
1 *or 2 wineglasses marsala*	*Thyme and Parsley*
1 *onion, chopped*	*Apples*
1 *carrot, chopped*	*Salt and pepper*
1 *stick celery, chopped*	2 *bayleaves*
2 *rashers bacon, chopped*	*Lentils*
6 *stoned green olives*	*White stock*

Truss the duck loosely as for roasting and rub inside and out with salt and bayleaves. Stuff with cored but not peeled apples.

Heat the olive oil in a large braising pan. Fry the bacon, onion, carrot and celery and then the duck, turning it so that it browns all over. Pour the wine over it and simmer until the wine evaporates. Add the parsley, thyme and olives and enough hot white stock or water to cover the bottom of the pan, and simmer gently until the duck is tender. Baste from time to time.

Cook the lentils in the usual manner, adding a little chopped garlic and celery. Mash to a purée, adding some of the gravy from the duck.

Remove the duck, scoop out the stuffing—this can be used as a garnish—rub the gravy and vegetables through a sieve, and serve separately as a sauce. Serve the duck surrounded by mashed lentils and the apple stuffing.

DUCK WITH NOODLES
PAPPARDELLE COLL' ANITRA

This dish, for which I think a rather ancient duck is adequate, is eaten in Florence on August 10th, the Feast Day of St. Lorenzo.

1 *duck*	*Salt and pepper*
1 *lb. tomatoes*	*Butter or oil*
2 *glasses red wine*	*Wide noodles*
Sage and rosemary	1 *teaspoon sugar*

Joint a prepared duck and rub it well with salt. Peel and chop the tomatoes and simmer them gently in butter or oil until they are soft. Add sugar, salt, pepper, sage and rosemary. Stir altogether and when the tomatoes are sufficiently soft, add the pieces of duck, as well as the heart, liver and gizzard finely chopped. Pour in the wine and simmer gently until the duck is tender. During cooking add, if necessary, either some more wine or hot stock to make a good sauce. Strip the meat from the duck pieces and chop very finely. Return the meat to the pan and cook for another ten minutes.

Cook the noodles in plenty of boiling, salted water until they are tender. The time depends on the size and the quality of the noodles, but they should not take more than fifteen to twenty minutes at the most. Drain well, then stir them into the duck sauce and serve immediately.

FIELDFARE

UCCELLETTI ALLA MAREMMANA

Italians and the Mediterranean peoples generally make far more use of their small birds than we do. In some Italian provinces many of the choicest dishes consist of these small birds. We are apt to be rather squeamish about them.

For this particular dish the birds are not drawn and their heads are left on. They are browned in hot olive oil, then peeled and chopped tomatoes, filleted anchovies, garlic and chopped green olives are added. The birds are then simmered gently until tender.

They are served on slices of crisply fried bread with their sauce.

In the Province of Grosseto, the place of origin of this recipe, the olives used are a special type of dried olive.

WILD DUCK

ANITRA SELVATICA

1 *wild duck*	*Salt and pepper*
Parsley	*Oil and butter*
Juice and rind of one orange	*Apple or celery*
1 *or* 2 *glasses marsala*	½ *clove garlic, chopped*

The flavour and treatment of wild duck depends much on the time of year and the duck's local feeding habits. If the flavour is mild, then it needs merely to be wiped with a damp cloth. If it is strong, then it should be well washed and stuffed with apple or celery, either of which will absorb the duck's strong flavour. This stuffing should be removed before serving the duck.

Heat some oil and butter in a roasting pan and place the duck, well brushed with olive oil, in the pan breast down. Bake in a moderate oven until tender, allowing about twenty minutes per pound. Baste from time to time with a marsala basting sauce. Duck, like wild goose, should not be overcooked as its flesh becomes dry and crumbly.

BASTING SAUCE. Heat in a small saucepan about two tablespoons of olive oil, add the parsley, garlic, salt and pepper and, when very hot, the marsala. Bring this quickly to the boil so that it will blend more easily, then add the orange juice and rind. Baste the duck with this fairly often and when the duck is cooked add, if liked, a little cream and some more marsala to the sauce and serve separately.

GAME BIRDS COOKED IN MARSALA
BECCAFICHI AL MARSALA

Intended for all kinds of small game birds. Also good for snipe and squabs.

12 *small game birds*	8 *filleted anchovies*
12 *stoned black olives*	6 *tablespoons white stock*
Enough oil for browning	*Juniper berry*
2 *cloves garlic, chopped*	1 *wineglass white wine*
1 *wineglass marsala*	*Slices of bread*
4 *peppercorns*	*Salt and pepper*
1 *tin Italian tomato paste*	

Clean the birds and rub them with salt and pepper and one crushed juniper berry. Heat the olive oil and brown the birds, then remove them from the pan, but keep them warm. Dilute the paste with the stock and gradually pour this into the pan in which you have browned the birds. Stir until the oil and the tomato stock are well blended, add the garlic, peppercorns, olives and anchovies and stir everything together before adding the white wine. Simmer for one or two minutes, then return the birds to the pan. Cover and cook very slowly until they are tender. Just before serving add a glass of marsala.

Fry until very crisp some slices of bread—one slice should do for two birds if the latter are very small. Place the birds on the bread, pour the sauce over birds and bread and serve immediately.

HARE IN SOUR-SWEET SAUCE
LEPRE IN AGRODOLCE

1 *hare*	2 *tablespoons olive oil*
1 *pint red wine*	1 *oz. butter*
1 *onion, chopped*	1 *oz. flour*
1 *carrot, chopped*	*Salt and black pepper*
1 *stick celery, chopped*	1 *oz. chocolate powder*
3 *juniper berries*	1 *breakfast cup thick cream*
2 *bayleaves*	2 *tablespoons sugar*
3 *cloves*	2 *tablespoons raisins*
¼ *stick cinnamon*	1 *tablespoon pine nuts*
3 *large sliced onions*	

Joint the hare, taking care not to break its bones. Save the blood and strain it into a bowl. Add the wine, the onion, carrot, celery, juniper berries, cloves, bayleaves and cinnamon. Put the pieces of hare into this mixture. See that they are well covered and then leave for twenty-four hours.

Next day heat the oil and butter, and fry the sliced onions until soft but not brown. Dredge with flour, stir this well into

the onions and cook gently for another five minutes. Remove
the hare from the marinade and add it to the onions. Take the
cinnamon from the marinade, then pour the rest into the pan
with the hare. Season very generously with salt and black
pepper and add one heaped tablespoonful of powdered chocolate—not cocoa—and stir this well into the sauce. Add the
sugar, pine nuts and raisins and continue to cook over a very
moderate heat for another thirty minutes. Add cream, reheat
but do not boil.

Other furred game can be cooked in this kind of sauce.
Although at first glance the combination of chocolate and
onions may seem startling it is not so. The taste of the chocolate is drowned by the many other flavours, and it serves more
to darken the sauce than anything else.

CASSEROLE OF PHEASANT
FAGIANO IN CASSERUOLA

1 *pheasant*	2 *wineglasses white wine*
Butter	1 *glass madeira*
Salt and pepper	*Pinch ground clove*
Small bunch muscat raisins	*Juniper berry (optional)*
2 *wineglasses brandy*	

Rub the pheasant inside and out with salt, brush with olive oil
and, if available, just a little crushed juniper. Put it into a
casserole with plenty of butter and brown, using the top of the
stove. Pour in the brandy, cover the pan and put it into the
oven. Baste from time to time.

While the pheasant is cooking make the following sauce.
Stem and stone the raisins and simmer in enough hot water to
cover, until plump. Drain thoroughly and put them into a
small saucepan with about one ounce of butter. Add the wines,
seasoning and ground clove. Simmer very gently for five

minutes. When the pheasant has been cooking for about thirty minutes, baste it with this sauce. Continue to cook the pheasant in the sauce, basting at least twice before cooking time is over. The average pheasant takes about forty-five minutes to cook in a covered casserole.

Serve the pheasant in the sauce and with chestnut purée.

CASSEROLE OF PIGEONS
PICCIONE SELVATICO ALL'USO UMBRO

This recipe is intended for wood pigeons and they can be simmered in a casserole for just as long as it takes to make them tender.

In an ordinary frying pan heat enough oil to fry the required number of pigeons, add salt and pepper and the juice of one whole lemon to each two or three pigeons. Prepare the pigeons as for roasting but leave the heads on and the giblets intact. Fry until brown. In a fireproof casserole heat a little more olive oil, add some slices of bacon—the quantity depends on your personal taste—add salt, pepper, some chopped sage and then the pigeons. Pour the oil in which they have been browning over them and then add two good-sized glasses of white wine. Simmer until the wine has been reduced, then add enough hot stock to cover completely the bottom of the casserole. Add more stock during cooking if necessary.

When tender, remove the pigeons from the casserole, chop off the heads, take out the giblets and joint the pigeons. Return the giblets to the casserole, add one or two anchovies, some chopped parsley, chopped capers and enough hot stock to turn all these ingredients into a sauce. Bring to the boil, then simmer for about ten minutes. Rub everything through a sieve, return to the casserole, add the pigeons, re-heat and serve hot. Serve with noodles, with rice or with well-creamed potatoes.

PIGEON RAGOUT
RAGU DI PICCIONE

2 or 3 *pigeons*	1 *or* 2 *wineglasses marsala*
1 *oz. bacon, chopped*	*Salt and black pepper*
1 *carrot, chopped*	2 *oz. butter*
1 *large onion, chopped*	2 *tablespoons oil*
1 *stick celery, chopped*	*Stock or water*
2 *tablespoons parsley, chopped*	*Cream or flour*
2 *tablespoons dried mushrooms, chopped*	

Joint the pigeons. Heat the butter and oil together in a braising pan and sauté the bacon, carrot, celery and onion. Add the pieces of pigeon, brown them all over, add parsley, salt and pepper, then cover with boiling stock or water. Throw in the mushrooms, previously soaked, and cook very slowly until the pigeons are tender. Pour in the marsala and simmer for another five minutes.

Remove the pigeons and arrange them on a large serving dish. Keep them hot. Rub the gravy and vegetables through a sieve, return this to the pan, add either cream or a thin flour and water paste, re-heat and then pour over the pigeons. Surround with a plain boiled rice and serve hot.

ROAST PIGEONS
PICCIONE ARROSTO

Italian pigeons are much plumper and more succulent than their British relatives. Properly jointed an Italian pigeon can be made to feed four.

Prepare the pigeons as you would roasting chickens, rubbing the breasts well with olive oil and larding them. Put into each pigeon a large piece of sage flavoured butter: this helps to keep them moist. Put them in a roasting tin with plenty of hot butter or oil, season with salt and pepper and bake in a moderate oven, basting frequently, for about half an hour or until the pigeons are tender. Just before they are ready remove the larding, baste again and leave them to brown. Avoid overcooking. Joint and serve on toast or well-fried bread.

If you prefer to serve the pigeons whole, stuff them first before roasting. Grated Parmesan cheese, breadcrumbs, chopped onion, raisins and pine nuts all make a good stuffing for pigeons.

Wild pigeons are not very good for roasting as they are usually far too tough.

If you do not care for sage, parsley butter can take its place.

RABBIT IN A 'FRYING PAN', ROMAN STYLE
CONIGLIO IN PADELLA

The best type of pan for this recipe is thick-bottomed, not too deep and having a tightly-fitting lid.

Wash and joint the rabbit and cut into convenient pieces for serving. Soak in cold water for several hours. Dry on a cloth and rub with salt, pepper and savoury herbs.

Heat enough oil in the pan to sauté the rabbit pieces, add one clove of sliced garlic, four rashers of bacon, one heaped teaspoon of chopped parsley and one wineglass of white wine. Simmer until the wine has disappeared and then add six chopped and peeled tomatoes and enough hot stock or water to prevent burning and for basting. Cover firmly, and cook very slowly until the rabbit is tender, basting from time to time.

Serve the rabbit with its sauce, and with a platter of risotto.

FRIED RABBIT
CONIGLIO FRITTO

Only a very young tame rabbit is suitable for frying. Clean it well, joint it neatly—or get the butcher to do this for you—and soak the pieces in cold water for several hours. Dry each piece with a cloth, then rub with lemon juice, salt and pepper.

Dice several rashers of fat bacon and fry in oil until very crisp. Add the rabbit pieces and brown lightly on both sides. Continue to fry gently until cooked through.

Serve very hot with a fresh watercress salad and thin slices of lemon garnished with red currant jelly.

The rabbit pieces may also be dipped in beaten egg and rolled in breadcrumbs before frying, or, if you are keen on batter, dip them first into a good coating batter and fry in deep, hot, bacon-flavoured olive oil.

Provided that the rabbit is tender it can be almost as good as chicken and is considerably cheaper.

RABBIT, HUNTER'S STYLE
CONIGLIO ALLA CACCIATORA

Clean, wash and joint a rabbit then leave it to marinate in burgundy or some other red wine for several hours.

Heat some olive oil and butter—enough to fry the rabbit in a fireproof casserole—and lightly fry one chopped onion, two sliced cloves of garlic, and the rabbit pieces previously well dried. Season with salt and pepper, add a little hot stock and simmer for forty minutes. Sprinkle with chopped rosemary, and then pour in the wine in which you marinated the rabbit. Continue to cook very slowly until the rabbit is tender, and if it is necessary to add more liquid, let it be warmed wine. Cover the casserole while cooking.

There are numerous recipes styled 'Hunter's'. This is a

simple one. Some add vegetables, others plenty of tomatoes, others treble the amount of onions, while some prefer sage to rosemary.

ROAST AND STUFFED RABBIT
CONIGLIO RIPIENO AL FORNO

1 *large tame rabbit*
Larding
2 *carrots, chopped*
2 *onions, chopped*
1 *stick celery, chopped*
1 *teaspoon sage, chopped*
Salt and pepper
Olive oil
Lemon juice
Vinegar

STUFFING:

2 *oz. veal*
2 *oz. beef*
2 *oz. dried mushrooms*
2 *oz. breadcrumbs*
Cream or milk
1 *tablespoon chopped parsley*
Butter

Clean the rabbit and wash it thoroughly in a mixture of vinegar and cold water. Leave it soaking in very cold water for several hours. Soak the mushrooms in tepid water for about twenty minutes. Drain them thoroughly and pat gently dry. Chop finely.

For the filling, put the meat through a mincer, mix with the mushrooms and the parsley, and fry lightly in butter for five minutes. Put this mixture into a bowl, add the breadcrumbs, salt and pepper, moisten with cream or milk, then knead to a paste.

Dry the rabbit on a cloth and rub inside and out with salt, pepper, sage and lemon juice. Fill the rabbit with the stuffing and sew it up or fix it firmly with skewers. Cover with larding and place it in a baking tin previously heated and well oiled. Surround the rabbit with the chopped vegetables, and bake it in a hot oven until the rabbit is browned, then reduce the heat and continue baking until the rabbit is tender, basting often with boiling water, or red wine and boiling water mixed.

Remove the rabbit from the pan, pass the gravy and the vegetables through a sieve. Put the sieved sauce into a saucepan, reheat, add a little boiling water or hot stock if available, skim off any excess fat and stir in a little cream just before serving. Serve the rabbit and the sauce separately.

RABBIT, IN A SOUR-SWEET SAUCE, SICILIAN STYLE
CONIGLIO AGRODOLCE

1 *rabbit*	*A little butter and oil*
1½ *bottles red wine*	1 *pint stock*
2 *onions, chopped*	*Salt and pepper*
2 *sprigs parsley*	1 *tablespoon sugar*
1 *sprig fresh thyme*	*Red wine vinegar*
4 *peppercorns*	1 *tablespoon sultanas*
1 *bayleaf*	1 *tablespoon pine nuts*
2 *cloves*	

Joint the rabbit, clean it well and leave it for several hours marinating in the red wine. Remove the rabbit, put the red wine into a saucepan and, if you have any, the blood from the rabbit. Add one onion, the cloves, parsley, thyme, peppercorns and bayleaf. Bring to the boil, and then pour this marinade over the rabbit pieces. Leave for thirty minutes.

Heat the butter and the oil in a fireproof casserole and lightly fry one onion and the rabbit pieces. Strain the marinade and, when the rabbit pieces are browned, pour the strained marinade into the pan and simmer until it has been considerably reduced. Gradually add the stock, some salt and pepper and continue to cook slowly until the rabbit is tender.

Take two or three tablespoonfuls of the liquid from the still

simmering rabbit and put this into a small saucepan. Add the
sugar and cook until this has completely melted. Pour in half
a glass of good quality red wine vinegar and stir everything
with a wooden spoon. Add the sultanas and pine nuts and
simmer for another five minutes. Pour this sauce over the
rabbit and stir it into the gravy. See that each piece of the
rabbit has some of the sweet sauce. Serve very hot.

RABBIT STEWED IN WINE
CONIGLIO IN UMIDO

Cut a rabbit into pieces as for Fried Rabbit (page 123), and
after washing them well, leave the pieces to soak for several
hours in cold water. Dry on a cloth, rub with salt, pepper and
sage. In a saucepan heat some oil, butter and bacon fat and
then sauté the rabbit pieces. Add plenty of chopped onion, at
least one pound of tomatoes, a glass of white wine, and simmer
until the wine has evaporated. Fill the pan three-quarters full
with hot stock or water, add salt and pepper and continue to
cook slowly until the rabbit is very tender.

Remove the rabbit pieces from the pan and put them into a
deep and hot serving dish. Thicken the stock with a thin flour
and water paste and cook for another five minutes. Pour the
vegetables and sauce over the rabbit and serve with potatoes
which have been boiled and then tossed in butter and chopped
parsley.

FILLETS OF TURKEY'S BREAST
FILETTI DI TACCHINO ALLA MODENESE

Slice the breast into fillets, each very thin, dip in beaten egg
and seasoned breadcrumbs and fry lightly in butter until a
golden brown.

Well butter an oven casserole—one of the kind which can

be used at table. Arrange some thin slices of bacon at the bottom, and cover them with slices of gruyère cheese and then the turkey fillets. Add another layer of bacon and cheese and bake in a hot oven until the cheese melts. Serve at once, well garnished with fried peppers and other green vegetables.

ROAST AND STUFFED TURKEY
TACCHINO RIPIENO ALLA LOMBARDA

Stuffed turkey is a great Italian favourite and it can be bought, not only at Christmas but on other Feast Days, trussed and stuffed and ready for the oven. Here is a stuffing from Lombardy.

• 4 oz. beef	2 wineglasses white wine
2 oz. veal or pork	Mace, rosemary and sage
4 oz. pork sausage	Salt and pepper
3 oz. prunes	Butter and oil
6 oz. grated cheese	Several rashers of bacon
2 lb. chestnuts	1 clove garlic
2 eggs	1 onion
1 turkey trussed and ready for stuffing	

Soak the prunes overnight, stone and chop. Cook the chestnuts until easily skinned, then re-boil and cook again until soft. Beat the eggs, mince the meats and the sausage, and chop the liver and gizzard as finely as possible. Mix all these ingredients together, add salt and pepper and fry very lightly in a little olive oil. Put into a bowl, add the cheese and the eggs, mash everything and then add a little white wine.

Push the stuffing into the neck and the body of the turkey. Sew up all apertures carefully. Heat plenty of butter in a roasting pan, add the onion coarsely sliced, garlic, mace, rosemary, sage and several rashers of bacon. Place the turkey on top of these ingredients and roast it until brown in a hot oven. Reduce the heat, baste once with the wine preferably heated, and then continue to roast it in a more moderate oven until it is tender, basting frequently with either boiling stock or water. Take out the garlic after twenty minutes' roasting.

When the turkey is tender take it from the pan, pass the gravy through a fine wire sieve and thicken it with a little cream or flour and water paste. Serve the turkey and the sauce separately and surround the turkey with boiled chestnuts.

QUAIL COOKED IN WINE
QUAGLIE AL VINO BIANCO

6 *quail* (*snipe, woodcock or plover*)	1 *pint white wine*
2 *small onions, chopped*	½ *pint thick cream*
2 *cloves garlic, chopped*	*Salt and black pepper*
1 *bayleaf*	*Butter or Italian olive oil*
6 *peppercorns*	*Raisins*
2 *cloves*	*Pine nuts*
	Croûtons

Clean, draw and truss the quails. Fill each with a few raisins previously soaked in hot water until plump, and pine nuts. Lard them well or brush generously with melted butter—quail can be very dry if not properly treated.

Heat enough oil or butter in a fireproof casserole to brown the quail. Sauté the onions, add the garlic, peppercorns, cloves, bayleaf and quail. Brown the latter all over, add salt and pepper, then pour in the wine. Cover and simmer gently for about half an hour, then put the quail on to a hot serving dish. Strain the gravy through a wire sieve, return it to the casserole to re-heat, and then stir the cream into it. Pour the sauce over the quail and serve them at once with fried croûtons.

VEGETABLES
ERBAGGI E LEGUMI

FRIED GLOBE ARTICHOKES
CARCIOFI ALLA GIUDIA

Much of the Roman cuisine is as seasonable as the weather.
With the spring come the fresh, small artichokes and this way
of cooking them is a Roman-Jewish speciality. Only very
young artichokes can be used, as every part of the vegetable,
including the choke, is eaten.

Wash the artichokes in salted water and drain, bottoms up.
Trim the leaves to a point with sharp scissors and in between
each leaf push some slivers of garlic. Fry in deep, boiling oil
and, while the artichokes are cooking, sprinkle them with salt
and pepper. Remove with a perforated spoon, drain free from
oil, spread out the leaves slightly to give the artichoke the
appearance of a flower, and serve with a vinegar dressing or
melted butter.

ARTICHOKES COOKED IN WINE
CARCIOFI ALLA ROMANA

Use very small and fresh artichokes, wash them in salted water
and drain—bottoms up. Trim the leaves to a point and push
chopped mint, parsley and salt well down between the leaves.

Heat a little oil and sauté the artichokes for a short while,
then add white wine or strained chicken stock—a pint of
either to one dozen artichokes. Continue to cook slowly until
the artichokes are tender and most of the liquid has evaporated.

Serve cold and with the remaining liquid.

ASPARAGUS PARMESAN
ASPARAGI ALLA PARMIGIANA

1 *lb. asparagus*	*Salt, pepper and nutmeg*
2 *oz. butter*	*Lemon juice*
Parmesan cheese	

Scrape the stalks of the asparagus, cut off any tough ends—
these can be used in soup—and wash in cold water. Tie in
bundles and place on the bottom of a large saucepan. Cover
with boiling water flavoured with lemon juice. Cook fairly
quickly until tender. Drain and arrange on a serving dish.
Sprinkle with salt, pepper and nutmeg. Melt the butter and
pour this over the asparagus, then sprinkle it with grated
Parmesan cheese.

This recipe is suitable for both green or white asparagus
and is, in fact, rather better with the thinner varieties.

FRIED ASPARAGUS
ASPARAGI FRITTI

1 *lb. cooked green asparagus*	*Salt and pepper*
1 *or 2 beaten eggs*	*Fat or oil for frying*
Breadcrumbs	*Flour*

Tie the asparagus in bundles of four stalks. Dip in seasoned
flour, then in eggs and breadcrumbs. Fry in deep, boiling fat or
oil until brown.

BAKED ASPARAGUS
ASPARAGI AL FORNO

Prepare asparagus as in penultimate recipe but cook for ten

minutes only in lemon-flavoured water. Drain, put into a well-buttered baking dish, season it with salt and pepper, pour over it plenty of melted butter and cover all but the tips with grated cheese, preferably Parmesan. Bake in a slow oven until tender—twenty minutes should be ample unless the asparagus is very tough. Sprinkle lightly with paprika pepper before serving.

FRIED AUBERGINE SLICES
MELANZANE FRITTE

4 *medium aubergine*	*Salt*
(*egg-plant*)	*Coating batter*

Wash the aubergine, cut off the stems, peel and slice thinly in rounds. Sprinkle the slices with salt and press between two plates. Leave for one hour. Wipe dry with a cloth and dip in coating batter. Fry in deep boiling fat until brown.

Alternatively you can dip the slices in egg and breadcrumbs, or fry *au naturel*. Serve hot.

AUBERGINE CASSEROLE WITH CHEESE
MELANZANE ALLA ROMANA

6 *aubergine* (*egg-plant*)	1 *pint stock*
½ *lb. cottage cheese*	*Oil for frying*
1 *small tin tomato paste*	*Salt, pepper and mustard*

Wash the aubergine, remove the stalks, peel and slice into thick rounds. Sprinkle with salt and press between two plates. Leave for one hour, wipe dry and fry *au naturel*. Arrange in layers in a greased oven casserole spreading cottage cheese between each layer. Thin the tomato paste with the stock, season with salt, pepper and mustard and pour this over the aubergine. Bake in a moderate oven for twenty minutes.

GREEN BEANS· IN TOMATO SAUCE
FAGIOLINI VERDI AL POMIDORO

2 *lb. green beans*
1 *tablespoon Italian tomato*
  paste
1 *grated onion*

1 *teaspoon sugar*
Juice of half a lemon
Salt and pepper
2 *oz. butter*

Wash the beans, and if they are very long break them into pieces. Cover with boiling water, add salt, and cook until tender. Drain well.

Heat the butter, lightly fry the onion, then add all the remaining ingredients, including the beans. Stir well so that each bean is well coated with the sauce, and simmer gently for about five minutes before serving.

BROCCOLI COOKED IN WINE
BROCCOLI AL VINO BIANCO

2 *lb. broccoli or cauliflower*
2 *wineglasses white wine*
1 *clove garlic*

Salt and pepper
½ *cup hot oil*

Cook the broccoli or cauliflower until almost tender. Drain and divide into flowerets.

Heat the oil, fry the garlic, remove it from the pan, add the flowerets and sauté to a golden brown. Add the wine and simmer until the flowerets are tender. Sprinkle with salt and pepper. Serve in the oil and and wine sauce.

A Sicilian recipe similar to this includes stoned olives and uses *vin rosé* instead of white wine. Just before serving, three or four anchovies are added.

FRIED BROCCOLI
BROCCOLI FRITTI

2 *lb. broccoli*	*Oil for deep frying*
1 *or* 2 *beaten eggs*	*Grated Parmesan cheese*
Flour	*Salt and pepper*

For this recipe one should use very firm green or mauve broccoli, with large heads.

Remove the green leaves, wash the broccoli and cook it in boiling salted water, with the heads clear of the liquid. Leave like this for twenty minutes then push the heads under the water and cook for another ten minutes. Drain and season with salt and pepper. Divide into flowerets, roll these in flour and dip into beaten egg. Fry until a golden brown in deep boiling oil.

Serve generously sprinkled with grated Parmesan cheese.

Cauliflower can be cooked in exactly the same way.

BRUSSELS SPROUTS
CAVOLINI DI BRUXELLES

2 *lb. Brussels sprouts*	1 *oz. butter*
1 *grated onion*	*Salt*
2 *oz. diced bacon*	*Grated Parmesan cheese*

Clean the sprouts, remove wilted leaves and soak them in cold water for thirty minutes. Wash well and cook in boiling, salted water until tender, but not soft. Drain very dry.

Heat the butter, fry the bacon and onion until brown, add the sprouts and toss them very gently in butter until a light amber colour. Serve with grated cheese.

Or omit the bacon, onion and cheese, and instead add half a pound of whole cooked chestnuts to the Brussels sprouts while frying them in butter. Serve the sprouts and the chestnuts together.

BRUSSELS SPROUTS WITH EGG SAUCE
CAVOLINI DI BRUXELLES IN SALSA

1 *lb. cooked Brussels sprouts*   3 *tablespoons white wine*
½ *pint meat stock*   *Salt and pepper*
2 *beaten eggs*   *Butter*

Heat the butter and slightly sauté the Brussels sprouts until they begin to change colour. In another pan warm the stock, season it and whisk the eggs into it. Simmer very gently until the mixture thickens. Take the sauce from the heat, whip it up, add the wine, whip again, then serve it poured over the sprouts. Ordinary runner or french beans are also excellent cooked in this way.

CABBAGE COOKED IN WINE
CAVOLI AL VINO BIANCO

1 *large white cabbage*   1 *cup white wine*
1 *grated onion*   *Salt*
1 *tablespoon capers*   1 *teaspoon sugar*
1 *cup boiling water*   2 *tablespoons oil or butter*

Wash the cabbage well, remove wilted leaves and cut it into quarters. Soak for thirty minutes in cold salted water. Thoroughly drain and shred.

Heat the oil in a saucepan, brown the onion, then toss the cabbage in the oil. Add water, salt and sugar and stir, then add the wine and capers. Stir everything together again, cover the pan and cook fairly slowly until the cabbage is tender. Fifteen minutes for a young cabbage and twenty-five for an older one should be enough. Drain the cabbage before serving, although there will not be much liquid.

CAULIFLOWER WITH LEMON SAUCE
CAVOLFIORE ALLA VILLEROY

1 *large cauliflower*   *Salt and pepper*
2 *beaten egg yolks*   1 *oz. flour*
Juice of half a lemon   1 *oz. butter*

Remove the outer leaves and thick stalk of the cauliflower and soak it in salted water, head down, for half an hour. Rinse, cover with salted water and cook until tender. Drain (reserving liquid) and keep hot.

Make a roux with the butter and flour and thin it with half a pint of the cauliflower stock. Beat the eggs and lemon together until frothy. Take the white sauce from the heat, whip in the egg and lemon mixture, add seasonings, re-heat, stirring all the time. Pour this sauce over the cauliflower before serving.

BRAISED FENNEL
FINOCCHI AL BURRO

1½ *lb. fennel*   2 *cups stock*
3 *oz. butter*   *Salt and pepper*

Wash and scrape the fennel and cut it into lengths. Simmer in butter until lightly browned. Add seasonings and meat stock and continue to cook gently until tender.

Another popular method of cooking fennel is to cook it slowly in stock until tender, then drain it well and arrange in a casserole. Sprinkle it generously with grated cheese, add salt and pepper and dredge lightly with fine breadcrumbs. Bake in a hot oven until the cheese has formed a thin crust.

Fennel is not unlike celery in appearance. It has thick fleshy leaves, and a crisp white bulb or root. Its flavour is vaguely that of aniseed, and is greatly appreciated in Italy. Although an acquired taste, it is generally liked by those who try it once or twice.

MUSHROOMS WITH CHEESE
FUNGHI ALLA PARMIGIANA

Peel, wash and trim as many mushrooms as required. They should be fairly large. Place them, gills up, in a greased baking dish and sprinkle over them white bread crumbs, grated Parmesan cheese, chopped parsley and just the smallest amount of chopped garlic. Season with salt and pepper, pour a little boiling water in the bottom of the pan, top each mushroom with a small piece of butter or brush with olive oil and bake in a moderate oven for between fifteen to twenty minutes.

STUFFED MUSHROOMS
FUNGHI RIPIENI

1 *lb. large mushrooms*	2 *oz. soft breadcrumbs*
½ *clove garlic, chopped*	1 *tablespoon tomato paste*
1 *onion, chopped*	*Few strips bacon*
2 *tablespoons parsley, chopped*	4 *oz. butter*
6 *oz. minced meat*	*Salt and pepper*

Wash the mushrooms and remove the stems. Heat the butter and gently simmer the mushrooms for five minutes. Remove from the pan and put them into a greased casserole.

Brown the meat and onion in the mushroom butter then add all the other ingredients except the bacon. Simmer for a few minutes then pile this mixture into the mushrooms. Cover each with a strip of bacon and bake for twenty minutes in a moderate oven.

SOUR-SWEET CARROTS
CAROTE IN SALSA AGRODOLCE

2 *lb. carrots*	1½ *oz. flour*
2 *tablespoons sugar*	*Carrot stock*
Salt and pepper	3 *tablespoons vinegar*
2 *oz. butter*	

Scrape or peel the carrots and slice either in rounds or lengthwise. Cook in boiling, salted water in a covered saucepan until tender. Do not use more water than is necessary. Drain and reserve the liquid.

Heat the butter, add the flour and stir to a roux. Add salt and pepper, then enough of the carrot stock to make a sauce. Add sugar and vinegar and continue to simmer gently until the sauce is thick and smooth. Stir the carrots into the sauce, simmering until they are thoroughly re-heated.

LEEKS AU GRATIN
'FLAN' DI PORRI

2 *lb. leeks*	*Salt, pepper and nutmeg*
2 *rashers bacon*	1 *oz. flour*
1 *cup cream or milk*	*Grated Parmesan cheese*
1 *or* 2 *beaten eggs*	2 *tablespoons oil*

Wash and trim the leeks, leaving as much of the green part as possible. Cook in boiling salted water until tender.

Heat the oil, dice and fry the bacon. Sprinkle with flour, add the cream—or milk—and cook until the sauce is smooth. Add salt, pepper and nutmeg. Take from the heat and beat in the egg or eggs.

Drain the leeks and turn them into a greased oven casserole. Pour the sauce over them, sprinkle generously with the grated cheese and bake until the cheese has browned.

STUFFED BABY MARROWS (COURGETTES)
ZUCCHINI RIPIENI

4 marrows (large courgettes) Breadcrumbs
1 onion, chopped Grated Parmesan cheese
4 oz. minced meat Salt and pepper
1 tablespoon parsley, chopped ½ cup oil
4 tomatoes, chopped

Wash the marrows and cook for ten minutes in boiling, salted water. Drain, slice in half lengthwise and scoop out the centres.

Heat the oil, lightly fry the onion and meat, add the parsley, tomatoes and scooped-out marrow pulp. Season with salt and pepper and simmer for fifteen minutes. Fill the marrow halves with this mixture, sprinkle with breadcrumbs and cheese and bake in a moderate oven for fifteen minutes.

CREAMED ONIONS
CIPOLLE ALLA CREMA

2 lb. small white onions Nutmeg
Wineglass white wine 1 tablespoon flour
Salt and pepper

Peel the onions and place them, whole, in a saucepan. Add salt
and pepper and cover with cold water. Cook uncovered for
twenty minutes. Mix the flour with water to a thin paste. Add
to the pan, stir until the sauce is thick, add the wine and a
good pinch of nutmeg and continue to cook for another ten
minutes. Excellent with mutton.

STUFFED ONIONS
CIPOLLE RIPIENE

6 *large onions*	1 *beaten egg*
½ *lb. potato purée*	*Salt and pepper*
1 *tablespoon tomato paste*	*Soft breadcrumbs*
4 *tablespoons grated cheese*	*Butter*

Peel the onions and cook in plenty of boiling water for fifteen
minutes. Drain and cool in cold water. Scoop out the centres,
leaving a shell of two or three layers of onion. Chop the
scooped-out onion and combine with the remaining ingredients except the breadcrumbs and butter. Refill the onions
with this mixture, sprinkle with breadcrumbs, dot with butter
and bake in a moderate oven for twenty-five minutes.

ONIONS COOKED IN WINE
CIPOLLE AL VINO BIANCO

1 *lb. onions*	½ *cup olive oil*
2 *wineglasses white wine*	*Thyme*
1 *clove garlic, sliced*	*Salt and pepper*

Peel and slice the onions. Heat the oil and fry the onions with
the garlic until they begin to brown. Add salt and pepper,
thyme and wine. Simmer gently until the onions are soft.

SOUR-SWEET ONIONS
CIPOLLE IN SALSA AGRODOLCE

Peel one pound of small onions and lightly brown them in a
mixture of hot oil and butter. Add a glass of wine or tarragon
vinegar, two heaped tablespoonfuls of sugar and cook until
the onions are soft.

ONION FLAN
'FLAN' DI CIPOLLE

4 *large onions*
Bacon rinds
¾ *cup cream or top of the milk*
2 *eggs*

¼ *cup olive oil*
Salt and pepper
Flour
½ *lb. short pastry*

Line a flan tin with the pastry, leaving a good rim to make a
neat edge. Bake 'blind' for a few moments.

Peel and slice the onions in rounds. Heat the oil, fry the
bacon rinds and remove these when crisp. Fry the onions until
a golden brown, sprinkle them with flour, and stir con-
tinuously. Add salt and pepper and gradually the cream. Continue to cook gently until the onions are creamy.

Remove the pan from the fire and cool the mixture a little.
Beat the eggs—yolks and whites separately. Whip the yolks
into the creamed onions, then fold in the whites. Pour this
mixture into the flan case and bake in a moderate oven for
twenty minutes. Serve as accompaniment to roast meat, or as a
main course with a green salad.

FRIED PEPPERS
PEPERONI FRITTI

Wash as many peppers as required, remove the stalks and cut

them into rounds. Cut out the core and wipe off all the seeds. Dip in beaten egg and fry in deep boiling oil until browned. These are excellent served with a sour-sweet sauce.

BAKED POTATO PUFF
FOCACCIA DI PATATE

2 *lb. potatoes*	*Sherry glass* acquavit (*or gin*)
2 *oz. butter*	2 *oz. sugar*
½ *pint boiling milk*	*Grated rind of one lemon*
2 *beaten egg whites*	*Salt*
2 *beaten egg yolks*	

Peel the potatoes, cut them into pieces of fairly equal size and cook in boiling salted water until very soft. Drain off the water and mash the potatoes until fluffy. Beat in the butter and milk, then the sugar, *acquavit*, salt, lemon rind and beaten yolks. Fold in the whites—very stiffly beaten, then pour the mixture into a buttered soufflé dish. Bake in a moderate oven for ten minutes and serve at once.

STUFFED BAKED POTATOES
PATATE FARCITE

Scrub as many large potatoes as required. Bake them in a hot oven until tender. While the potatoes are cooking prepare a stuffing. Combine some finely minced meat, chopped parsley, soft breadcrumbs, grated cheese, salt, pepper and enough beaten egg to bind the mixture.

Cut the potatoes lengthwise if they are very large or, if only of medium size, slice off the top, and scoop out the insides. Mash this with hot milk and butter and beat to a cream. Combine with the meat mixture and pile lightly into the potato shells. Place in a baking tin and cover each potato half with a thin slice of cheese. Bake in a moderate oven for about fifteen minutes or until the cheese has formed a light brown crust.

SCALLOPED POTATOES
PATATE AL FORNO

1 *lb. potatoes*	1 *tablespoon chopped parsley*
½ *lb. courgettes (baby marrows)*	*Grated cheese*
1 *large chopped onion*	*Salt and pepper*
3 *large tomatoes*	*Brown breadcrumbs*
1 *clove garlic, chopped*	*Oil*

Clean and peel all the vegetables and cut them into slices. Rub a pie dish, or a casserole, with oil leaving a filmy layer at the bottom. Arrange all the vegetables in alternate layers, add the garlic—very finely chopped—salt and pepper. Sprinkle each layer with cheese, parsley and breadcrumbs. Pour a little oil or melted butter over the top layer. Sprinkle lightly with cheese and breadcrumbs to form a thin crust and bake in a moderate oven until all the vegetables are quite soft.

PUMPKIN, SICILIAN STYLE
ZUCCA GIALLA ALLA SICILIANA

2 *lb. pumpkin*	2 *teaspoons olive oil*
2 *wineglasses white wine*	2 *tablespoons lemon juice*
2 *sprigs mint*	½ *cup cream*
1 *teaspoon sugar*	*Salt*
1 *clove garlic (optional)*	

Peel the pumpkin, cut it into julienne slices, sprinkle with salt and leave for one hour.

Heat the oil in a saucepan, add the garlic, then the pumpkin. Brown a little, add the wine, sugar and mint and simmer gently until the pumpkin is tender but not squashy. Just before it is ready remove the mint, add the cream and lemon juice and continue to cook for another five minutes, stirring carefully all the time.

PURÉE OF DRIED PULSES (PEAS, BEANS, ETC.)
CREMA DI PISELLI, FAGIOLI LENTICCHIE

1 *pint any type mixed pulses*	1 *hard-cooked egg yolk*
1 *onion, chopped*	*Salt and pepper*
1 *stick celery, chopped*	2 *cloves*
1 *carrot, chopped*	1 *clove garlic*
1 *tomato, chopped*	*Pinch bicarbonate soda*
Bacon rinds	*Dry mustard*

Wash the pulses, cover with water and leave to soak overnight. Drain, cover again with cold water and bacon rinds, vegetables, cloves, soda and garlic. Cook slowly until soft. Strain and rub everything through a sieve to a purée. Mash the egg yolk with salt, pepper and mustard and beat this into the purée. Continue beating until it is smooth and creamy.

Serve topped with slices of crisply fried onions and triangles of fried bread.

Chick peas are particularly good cooked in this way.

SPINACH WITH CHEESE
SPINACI ALLA PARMIGIANA

Fry in butter for fifteen minutes some cooked and chopped spinach, season with salt and pepper and flavour with nutmeg and grated Parmesan cheese.

SPINACH WITH ANCHOVIES
SPINACI ALL' ACCIUGHE

2 *lb. spinach*   5 *anchovies*
1 oz. *butter or oil*   1 *clove garlic, chopped*
Pepper

Wash the spinach and cook it without water or salt until soft. Drain and chop finely.

Heat the butter, add the anchovies and garlic and sauté for a few moments. Return the spinach to the pan, add pepper, stir and cook until the spinach is quite re-heated. Serve with triangles of fried bread.

Salt is not necessary as the anchovies provide enough.

SPINACH FLAN
'FLAN' DI SPINACI

2 *lb. spinach*   1 *large onion, finely chopped*
2 oz. *butter*   *Salt and pepper*
½ *pint cream or top of milk*   *Grated nutmeg*
2 oz. *flour*   2 oz. *grated Parmesan cheese*
2 *well beaten eggs*   ½ *lb. short pastry*

Make a flan case of short pastry and bake it 'blind'. Wash and pick over the spinach and partly cook it without water. Drain and chop finely.

Heat the butter and fry the onion to a golden brown. Sprinkle with flour, stir and cook for three minutes before pouring in the cream or the top of the milk. Season well with salt and pepper and continue cooking very gently until the mixture is smooth and thick. Add the spinach and continue cooking until it is quite soft.

Remove from the fire, leave to cool, then beat in the cheese and eggs. Pour this mixture into the flan case, flavour slightly with nutmeg and bake in a hot oven for about fifteen to twenty minutes. Serve very hot.

SPINACH ROMAN STYLE
SPINACI ALLA ROMANA

Fry some cooked and chopped spinach in bacon fat with raisins, pine nuts, salt, pepper, spices and a very little chopped onion for fifteen minutes.

TOMATOES STUFFED WITH RICE
POMIDORI RIPIENI DI RISO

8 *tomatoes*	1 *stick celery, chopped*
6 *oz. rice*	1 *carrot, chopped*
Parsley, chopped	*Salt and pepper*
1 *clove garlic, chopped*	*Mint*
A little butter or oil	1 *teaspoon sugar*
1 *onion, chopped*	*Grated cheese*

Wash the tomatoes, cut off the tops and scoop out the centres. Sprinkle the cases with salt, pepper and chopped mint.

Heat the butter, or oil, and fry the onion, celery, carrot, parsley, garlic and scooped-out tomato. Simmer until soft, then pass this mixture through a sieve, add the sugar and the rice. Half fill each tomato case with the rice, top with grated cheese and place in a baking tin. Pour into the tin enough boiling water to reach half-way up the sides of the tomatoes. Bake very slowly in a moderate oven until the rice has cooked. If allowed to cook too quickly the rice will be hard and the tomatoes squashy.

6

If time is limited use cooked rice but in this case fill the tomato cases to the top.

TOMATO FLAN
FOCACCIA DI POMIDORO

2 lb. tomatoes	Pepper and salt
2 large onions, chopped	Sage
1 large courgette, sliced	1 teaspoon sugar
Bacon rinds	1 clove garlic, chopped
Chopped parsley	3 tablespoons oil
1-2 beaten eggs	¾ lb. short pastry
Grated Parmesan cheese	

Make enough short pastry to line a ten-inch flan case and bake it 'blind' for five minutes.

Heat the oil and fry the bacon rinds with the onions and garlic. Remove the rinds when they are crisp. Add the tomatoes, peeled and sliced, plenty of parsley, courgette, salt, pepper, sugar and a little sage. Simmer until everything is soft.

Pour this mixture into the flan case. Cover the top with the egg and sprinkle it with grated cheese. Bake in a fairly hot oven until the pastry is a golden brown.

BUTTERED TURNIPS
RAPE AL BURRO

Peel as many turnips as required and cut into thin rounds. Cook them gently in lightly salted, boiling water for twenty minutes. Drain and fry in butter on both sides.

When they are a golden brown, just before serving, sprinkle generously with grated cheese, preferably Parmesan.

EGG AND CHEESE DISHES
LE UOVA E PIATTI DI FORMAGGIO

𝕏⚜⚜⚜⚜⚜⚜⚜⚜⚜⚜⚜⚜⚜⚜⚜⚜⚜⚜⚜⚜𝕏

EGG AND CHEESE CREAM
FONDUTA

4 *egg yolks*	1 *oz. butter*
12 *oz. Fontina cheese, cut into*	*Fried bread*
cubes	*White pepper*
Milk	1 *white truffle (optional)*

This is Piedmont's most celebrated dish and must be made
with Fontina cheese, one of Italy's great cheeses. In appearance
it resembles Gruyère, with a firm texture and small eyes.
Fonduta must have Fontina cheese to be genuine.

Soak the cheese in milk for several hours. Put the butter and
the egg yolks into the top of a double pan and when the butter
begins to change colour add the cheese. Stir until the cheese is
completely melted, using a wooden spatula and never allowing
the mixture to boil. When it is thick and creamy remove from
the fire and add pepper. No salt is needed as the cheese con-
tains enough. In Piedmont white truffles, which are plentiful,
are added towards the end of cooking time.

Serve in individual bowls with fingers of fried bread.

EGGS FRIED WITH CHEESE
UOVA ALLA PARMIGIANA

Grease with bacon fat as many individual frying pans as required and drop one raw egg in each. Add plenty of salt,

pepper and diced bacon, and completely smother each egg with grated Parmesan cheese. Cook gently until the eggs are set, but not hard. Serve with fingers of fried bread.

POACHED EGGS WITH SALAD CREAM
UOVA AFFOGATE SUI CROSTINI

4 *eggs*
1 *oz. butter*
1 *wineglass white wine*

4 *slices toast*
Salad cream

Melt the butter in a small saucepan, add the wine and blend the two well. Break each egg separately in a cup and slip them, one at a time, into the wine. Poach each singly until the whites are firm. Carefully place each egg on a slice of toast and pour over each some fairly thin salad cream. Serve hot.

EGGS COOKED IN SWEET-SOUR SAUCE
UOVA IN SALSA AGRODOLCE

6 *eggs*
1 *onion, chopped*
2 *bayleaves*
2 *cloves*
Wineglass white wine
½ *pint stock*

1 *tablespoon sugar*
Salt and pepper
2 *oz. butter*
Flour
1 *tablespoon vinegar*

Cook the eggs for six minutes exactly in boiling water, then plunge into cold water and you will find them fairly easy to peel, even though they are not hard-boiled.

Heat the butter and simmer the onion until soft. Sprinkle with flour, add salt and pepper, stir until smooth then gradu-

ally pour in the stock. Add cloves and bayleaves and simmer
for fifteen minutes. Strain through a fine sieve. Re-heat, add
the sugar, vinegar, wine, then the eggs. Simmer until the eggs
are hard. Serve the eggs in the sauce with fried bread.
Eggs are equally good cooked this way in a tomato sauce.

EGGS WITH PEAS AND TOMATOES
UOVA COI PISELLI E POMIDORI

Rather similar to the previous recipe. Fry in oil or butter a
large chopped onion, one clove of garlic and a pound of sliced
tomatoes until very soft. Add a pound of cooked green peas,
salt and pepper, six cooked shelled eggs, sprinkle with paprika
and continue to cook until the eggs are set. An alternative way
is to put the cooked peas and tomatoes into a casserole, make
hollows into which to drop the eggs, sprinkle them with
paprika pepper and bake them in a moderate oven until they
are set.

EGGS, HUNTER'S STYLE
UOVA ALLA CACCIATORA

6 *eggs*	*Rosemary, basil and thyme*
6 *chicken livers*	*Salt and pepper*
1 *tablespoon chopped green olives*	*Butter*
	Flour
1 *small onion, grated*	6 *slices toast spread with liver*
Wineglass white wine	*paté*
¼ *pint tomato juice*	

Cut the livers into very small pieces and sauté them in butter.
Add the onion, brown it and very lightly dust with flour.
Stir and simmer for five minutes. Pour in the tomato juice, stir

this well into the livers and onion, then add wine, herbs, olives and seasonings. Mix all these ingredients well, then add the eggs one by one. Continue to cook slowly until the eggs are set. Place eggs and livers on toast and cover with sauce.

EGGS BAKED IN RICE
UOVA SUL RISO

6 eggs	1 *small onion, chopped*
8 oz. rice	3 oz. *Parmesan cheese, grated*
½ lb. *tomatoes, chopped*	*Salt, pepper, butter for frying*

Throw the rice into salted, boiling water, and cook until tender. Drain. Fry the onion in butter until brown, add the tomatoes and cook them until soft. Stir to a pulp, add salt and pepper and rub through a sieve. Mix the rice, cheese and sauce together and turn this mixture into a greased and fairly shallow casserole. Make six hollows in the rice, drop an egg into each, sprinkle with salt, pepper and extra Parmesan cheese. Bake in a moderate oven until the eggs are firm.

EGGS WITH SPINACH
UOVA FIORENTINA

2 lb. *cooked spinach*	6 *anchovies, chopped*
6 eggs	*Salt, black pepper and paprika*
6 oz. *Parmesan cheese, grated*	*pepper*

Chop the spinach finely, and put it into a shallow, buttered casserole—preferably oblong in shape. Make six small wells in the spinach and drop an egg into each. Add seasonings. Garnish with anchovies and sprinkle with cheese. Bake in a medium oven until the eggs are set.

You can use individual ramekin dishes instead of a casserole. if you prefer it.

EGGS POACHED IN TOMATO SAUCE
UOVA AL POMIDORO

4 eggs	2 tablespoons chopped parsley
1 lb. tomatoes	Salt and pepper
4 slices toast	Butter

Peel and slice the tomatoes and simmer in butter with the parsley until soft. Add salt and pepper and stir. Make four wells in the tomato pulp and drop an egg into each. Continue cooking until the eggs are set. Serve each egg on a slice of toast and cover with sauce.

EGGS IN TOMATO CUPS
UOVA ALLA CASALINGA

6 eggs	Salt and black pepper
6 large tomatoes	Butter

Scoop out the centres of the tomatoes and bake them in a moderate oven until they are almost soft, then drop an egg into each tomato. Sprinkle with salt and pepper, dot with butter and continue to bake until the eggs are set.

OMELETTE
FRITTATA

In Italy there are two distinct types of omelette as well as the many different flavourings for them. The first, the omelette proper, is made and folded like the French omelette. The second, and more usual version, is called a *frittata* and is not folded when cooked.

6 *eggs*	2 *oz. butter for frying*
2 *tablespoons milk*	*Salt and pepper*

Beat the eggs very slightly and combine with the milk and seasonings. Heat the butter in an omelette pan, pour just a little of it into the eggs, then pour the egg mixture into the pan. As the omelette begins to cook underneath, prick it with a fork and run a knife around the edges. When the underneath is a golden brown, fold the omelette over, and leave to set for one minute, then serve at once.

For flavouring combine the beaten eggs with any of the usual omelette flavourings, including chopped fresh mint, tarragon, chopped chervil, parsley, shallots, chives, onion and carrot. Cottage cheese is a very usual Italian omelette ingredient, also dried mushrooms, dandelion tips, asparagus and, of course, cheese of all types.

The *frittata* is made with eggs beaten very lightly—just enough to mix the whites and the yolks. A little milk is added, also salt and pepper and melted butter. When it has been freid to a golden brown on one side, it is turned over, as with a pancake, and fried on the other side. Its texture is not unlike that of a scrambled egg.

I find it easier to brown the top of a *frittata* under a grill as turning requires considerable knack and skill.

With a *frittata* rather more unusual fillings are used. Here are just a few.

OMELETTE
WITH CHEESE AND TOMATOES
FRITTATA ALLA CAMPAGNOLA

Beat four eggs very lightly. Mix with grated cheese, salt and pepper. Heat two ounces of butter in an omelette pan and fry until soft six peeled and chopped tomatoes. Flavour them with chopped mint, then pour over them the beaten eggs. Continue as instructed for *frittata*.

MACARONI OMELETTE
FRITTATA CON MACCHERONI ALLA NAPOLITANA

4 oz. cooked macaroni	1 teaspoon capers
4 eggs	Salt and pepper
2 tablespoons cream	Grated Parmesan cheese
Handful parsley, chopped	Butter for frying

Lightly beat the eggs, adding cream, salt and pepper.

Heat some butter in a large omelette pan and very lightly fry the macaroni. Add parsley, cheese, and capers and then stir in the eggs. Cook on top of the stove until the egg mixture is firm, then put under the grill to get a good, almost crusty, top.

OMELETTE, SAVOY STYLE
FRITTATA ALLA SAVOIARDA

Beat lightly four eggs with salt and pepper and add a little milk. Fry lightly in butter three tablespoonfuls of cold cooked potato, cut into cubes, and the same amount of bacon and gruyère cheese. Continue as above.

BAKED CHEESE OMELETTE
FRITTATA CON FORMAGGIO AL FORNO

Break four egg yolks in a basin and combine them with three

tablespoonfuls of milk. Beat very lightly. Whisk the whites until stiff and fold them into the egg yolks. Add two table-spoonfuls of grated gruyère cheese and pour the mixture into a well-buttered, shallow oven casserole. Bake in a moderate oven until a golden brown.

BREADCRUMB OMELETTE

FRITTATA ALLA CROSTINA

Beat lightly four eggs, adding salt and pepper but no milk. Sauté three tablespoonfuls of white breadcrumbs in butter, cover with two tablespoonfuls of cream, then add the beaten eggs. Continue as usual for *frittata*.

FRIED BREAD, NEAPOLITAN STYLE

CROSTINI ALLA NAPOLETANA

Fry several peeled and chopped tomatoes, with some finely chopped green peppers, flavour them with marjoram, salt and pepper and simmer until the tomatoes are very soft. Fry in butter as many slices of bread as required and brown both sides. Remove from the pan and keep hot. In the same butter fry an equal number of mozzarella cheese slices on both sides and put a slice of cheese on each slice of bread. Cover the cheese and bread with tomato sauce and serve very hot.

MOZZARELLA CHEESE SANDWICHES

MOZZARELLA IN CARROZZA

Cut as many thin slices of bread as required, trim off the crusts and spread with melted butter. Make sandwiches in the usual way, using mozzarella cheese as a filling. Press the edges together very firmly. Beat one or two eggs, adding salt and pepper, and dip the sandwiches in the beaten egg. Fry on both sides until brown in either very hot butter or oil.

If mozzarella is not available, use Bel Paese for these sandwiches. Instead of a coating of beaten egg, a coating of batter may be used.

TOMATO PIE

PIZZA ALLA NAPOLETANA

1 *lb. flour*	4 *oz. mozzarella cheese*
1 *oz. dried yeast*	*Marjoram, finely chopped*
2 *lb. tomatoes*	*Olive oil*
6 *filleted anchovies*	*Salt and pepper*
1 *clove garlic, chopped*	

Dissolve the yeast in a little tepid water. Mix the flour with one tablespoon of olive oil, then add to the dissolved yeast. Knead until the dough is smooth. Leave it in a bowl, covered, in a warm place for two hours or until it has doubled its bulk.

Peel and chop the tomatoes. Heat two tablespoons of oil in a pan; add the tomatoes, garlic, salt and pepper. Cook gently for thirty minutes or until soft.

When the dough has risen, roll it out lightly and spread it over a large well-oiled flat baking tin. The edges should be slightly thicker than the middle. Make slight indentations in the pastry. Spread it with the tomatoes. Slice the mozzarella and spread this over the top and garnish with anchovies. Bake in a very hot oven for ten minutes, reduce the heat to moderate and bake five to ten minutes longer.

This is the most usual of the *pizza* which is today as popular outside of Italy as within the country. The word simply means pie, therefore it is not surprising that the recipes vary enormously, so do pies. There are *pizze* with onions and bacon,

with cheese and tomatoes, with garlic and herbs. There are
those with fish filling, and some which are sweet. Some are
covered but most *pizze* are open, like a tart. There are also
pizze which are made at home with puff or flaky pastry;
these are usually called *alla casalinga,* or home-made.

CHEESE TART
PIZZA ALLA CAMPOFRANCO

Roll out fairly thinly half a pound of brioche pastry (page 167),
and spread it over a greased baking sheet. Cover with thin
slices of Mozzarella cheese, sliced bacon and tomatoes. Sprinkle
with grated Parmesan cheese. Beat one or two eggs with salt
and pepper until frothy and pour the mixture over the cheese.
Bake in a moderate oven until brown.

PIE WITH YEAST PASTRY
PIZZADALINA

Yeast dough from the baker	*Anchovies*
2 lb. onions	*5 oz. black olives*
Butter	*3 cloves garlic*
Parmesan cheese	*Salt and pepper*
Bayleaves, thyme, parsley	

Enough yeast dough is needed so that when pulled out it will
cover a fairly large, round, baking tin.

Peel and slice the onions and cook them in butter until they
are very soft. Try to keep them white. Add the garlic and the
herbs and remove these when the onions are cooked. Season
with salt and pepper. Prick the dough all over with a fork,
then cover it with the cooked onions. Add the olives, stoned
and halved, then decorate the pie with fillets of anchovy. Bake

the pie in a hot oven until a golden brown. It should take about thirty minutes.

If it is impossible to get dough from the baker, a puff pastry can be used instead.

EASTER CAKE
TORTA PASQUALINA

Flour	½ *lb. curd cheese*
1 *lb. beet leaves*	⅓ *pint fresh cream*
6 *eggs*	*Oil*
Handful chopped parsley	2 *oz. butter*
1 *chopped onion*	*Salt and pepper*
3 *oz. grated Parmesan cheese*	*Marjoram*

Mix one pound of sieved flour with one dessertspoonful of olive oil and enough warm water to make a smooth and pliable dough. Divide this into thirty pieces, shape them into balls, and leave them for one hour in a cool place, well covered with a damp cloth.

Cut away the spine from each of the beet leaves, then roll each one separately as when rolling cigarettes, then with sharp kitchen scissors cut each roll into pieces, roughly a quarter of an inch wide. Unroll each piece—they will look like noodles—wash them well and leave them to dry.

Heat the butter, very lightly fry the leaves, add the parsley, salt, pepper, onion, Parmesan cheese and marjoram. Leave this on the side of the stove until needed.

Beat into the curd cheese three tablespoonfuls of sieved flour, and when this mixture is smooth dilute it with the cream, and a few drops of olive oil. Put aside until needed, covered with a cloth.

Roll out separately fifteen of the balls of dough. Each should be the same size and rolled as thinly as possible. Grease a flat baking tin, and line the bottom with one of the pieces of dough. Brush this lightly with olive oil and cover it with another piece of dough. Continue to do this until all the fifteen pieces are neatly piled up one upon the other.

Spread the top layer with the beet mixture, cover this with the curd cheese. With the back of a spoon make 'wells' in the cheese and into each 'well' drop one raw egg. In between the eggs place thin slivers of butter.

Roll out the remaining piecesof dough, and pile these on top of the rest, brushing each layer with olive oil. Trim round the sides and with the pieces make an edge for the top layer. Prick the top with a fork to prevent blistering and bake in a moderate oven for one hour.

SALADS
INSALATA

CABBAGE SALAD
INSALATA DI CAVOLI

Wash well one small white cabbage and cook in slightly-salted water. Drain it and shred it finely.

Rub a wooden salad bowl with garlic and add the shredded cabbage.

Make a dressing with three parts Italian olive oil, one part tarragon vinegar and salt and black pepper to taste. Gradually add two well-beaten eggs and one cup of cream. Cook the dressing very slowly over boiling water until it thickens.

Pour the dressing while still hot over the cabbage and leave to cool. Garnish with anchovies and crisply fried parsley.

For successful frying, parsley must be very fresh and crisp. Drop into deep boiling fat for just one minute. If you tie a piece of cotton to the stems it makes it easier to pull the parsley quickly out of the fat when it is done.

CELERY SALAD
INSALATA DI SEDANO

Thoroughly wash and chop a head of celery, or, better still, just the heart, and the same amount of endive. Mix with a dressing of oil and vinegar and sprinkle with two tablespoonfuls of Italian *prosciutto* or its equivalent. Chill, and just before serving add a tablespoonful of home-made salad cream. Add salt and pepper to taste.

CHICORY SALAD
INSALATA DI CICORIA

Wash two crisp heads of chicory, remove any bruised or broken leaves, then chop the rest into small rounds. Mix with a little sliced garlic, some chopped green olives and Italian dressing (page 189).

In Italy, and especially in Piedmont, chopped white truffles are added. But in Britain or elsewhere a few green peas can add flavour and colour to the salad, or a teaspoonful of chopped, hot red peppers can be used.

CHRISTMAS EVE SALAD
INSALATA DI RINFORZ

Very thoroughly wash a large, white cauliflower and soak it head down for thirty minutes in cold, salted water. Divide it into flowerets and cook for ten to fifteen minutes in boiling salted water. Put the flowerets into a salad bowl previously rubbed with garlic, then pour over them enough Italian salad dressing (page 189) to coat each piece. Toss briskly, but not so violently that the cauliflower becomes mashed, then add six stoned black olives and one heaped tablespoonful of capers.

Chill before serving.

It is usual to serve this salad with carp or eel, and in Naples it is served on Christmas Eve.

FENNEL SALAD
INSALATA FINOCCHI

Select two very white and crisp bulbs of fennel. Trim and slice them into lengths—they should be rather thin. Toss lightly in salad oil and serve cold.

GIPSY SALAD
INSALATA GIPSY

1 *red*, 1 *green* and 1 *yellow* *pepper*	4 *anchovies*
1 *peeled tomato*	2 *tablespoons capers*
1 *onion*	1 *sprig fresh basil*
1 *stick celery*	1 *sprig fresh mint*
1 *head chicory*	1 *clove garlic chopped,*
4 *radishes*	*Pepper and dry mustard*
	½ *cup olive oil*

Chop the vegetables and anchovies and toss them very lightly with a wooden spoon. Add herbs, garlic, capers and seasonings, then gradually the olive oil. Chill and serve with boiled meats.

LETTUCE SALAD
INSALATA DI LATTUGHE

To make a good lettuce salad all the ingredients must first be chilled. Only wash the lettuce if it is absolutely necessary and, if you do, make sure it is perfectly dry. This can be done either in the conventional French lettuce dryer or by drying with a linen cloth. Pull the lettuce apart with your hands, do not use a knife.

Have ready a wooden salad bowl and rub it lightly first with salt, then with cut garlic, of this as much or as little as you please. Put the lettuce in the bowl and sprinkle it with finely-grated onion and black pepper. Pour over it a plain olive oil and tarragon vinegar dressing and toss briskly until each leaf is coated with the dressing.

If you want a crisp salad serve at once. But if you prefer, as many continental people do, a rather wilted affair, then leave it for a short while before serving.

HARICOT BEAN SALAD
INSALATA DI FAGIOLINI

Soak half a pound of haricot beans overnight. Next day cook them until soft in unsalted water to which a coffeespoon of bicarbonate of soda has been added. Drain, and remove any beans that are too soft and dry.

Chop very finely one small onion, one clove of garlic, a little sage, parsley, tarragon, sweet basil and rosemary and mix with one heaped tablespoonful of tinned tunny fish. Toss all this together with a spoon then, add three tablespoonfuls of olive oil and one of vinegar mixed together.

Mix this dressing with the beans, sprinkle with pepper and serve garnished with strips of anchovy.

VEGETABLE SALAD
CAPPON MAGRO

SALAD
1 small cauliflower
¼ lb. green peas
½ lb. French beans
½ lb. potatoes
4 carrots
1 stick celery
A few radishes
¼ lb. mushrooms
1 clove garlic
1 large arrowroot biscuit
Mixed fish (optional)

DRESSING
2 tablespoons chopped parsley
¼ lb. grated fennel (optional)
4 tablespoons capers
8 anchovies, chopped
2 hardboiled egg yolks
2 tablespoons soft breadcrumbs
Oil and lemon
Salt and pepper

Cook all the vegetables until tender. Divide the cauliflower into clusters, slice the carrots, potatoes, radishes and mushrooms.

Break the beans into halves and chop the celery. Rub a large arrowroot biscuit with garlic and, using this as a base, arrange all the vegetables on top, pyramid fashion, making an effective display of colour. In between, if available, put pieces of lobster, or shrimps, anchovies, smoked salmon or even smoked oysters.

Pound the garlic to a paste, add the remaining ingredients for the dressing and continue to pound until all are well blended and the paste is smooth. Gradually add oil and lemon and work the paste to a cream. Pour this over the salad. Surround the base with more lobster, shrimps, etc.

TUSCAN SALAD (BREAD SALAD)
'PANZANELLA' ALLA MARINNA

2 *slices white bread*	4 *anchovies*
Chopped fresh basil	2 *chilli peppers*
Handful chopped parsley	2 *cloves garlic*
1 *tablespoon capers*	*Salt and black pepper*
Tarragon vinegar	*Oil*

Soak the bread in water, squeeze it quite dry and crumble it finely. Mix with basil, parsley, capers, salt and pepper and just enough oil and vinegar mixed to moisten it. Put this aside while you prepare the dressing.

Pound the garlic to a paste, add the anchovies and peppers and continue pounding to a smooth paste. Work some vinegar into this until it is a creamy, but fairly thin, dressing.

Arrange the bread salad on a plate, surround it with slices of hardboiled egg or sliced tomato, pour the dressing over the salad, chill and serve.

Give this salad a trial, even though it seems unusual at first sight. It is typical of Mediterranean salads, really very good, and rather a welcome change from the eternal lettuce, tomato and radishes.

ITALIAN POTATO SALAD
INSALATA DI PATATE

8 *potatoes cooked in their skins*　　*Salt and pepper*
1 *large onion, chopped*　　2 *lettuce hearts*
2 *hardboiled eggs, chopped*　　1 *clove garlic*
1 *green pepper, chopped*　　*Italian dressing*
4 *anchovies, chopped*

Peel the potatoes and cut them into cubes or slices. Mix with the next five ingredients and add a little dressing. Wash and dry the lettuces, separating the leaves. Rub a bowl with garlic, put the lettuce at the bottom, add a little dressing, toss until all the leaves are well coated, then cover with potato salad.
Chill before serving.

SWEET-SOUR POTATO SALAD
INSALATA DI PATATE AGRODOLCE

6 *large potatoes cooked in their*　　3 *rashers diced bacon*
　　skins　　4 *oz. sugar*
1 *onion, chopped*　　*Salt and pepper*
1 *stick celery, chopped*　　½ *cup tarragon vinegar*
2 *hardboiled eggs, chopped*　　2 *beaten eggs*
1 *gherkin, chopped*　　¼ *teaspoon dry mustard*
1 *tablespoon parsley, chopped*　　*Oil for frying*

Peel the potatoes and either slice them or cut into cubes. Mix with the onion, celery, hardboiled eggs, gherkin and parsley.
Blend the vinegar with the beaten eggs and blend in half a cup of water. Add the sugar, salt, pepper and mustard. Heat a

little oil and fry the bacon until crisp, then add the egg and
vinegar mixture. Simmer over boiling water until the mixture
thickens, stirring all the while to prevent curdling. Pour it over
the potato salad while still hot, toss lightly and serve.

ONION SALAD
INSALATA DI CIPOLLE

Boil in salted water as many onions as required until they are
almost tender. Drain, cut into slices and leave to dry. Pour
over them enough Italian dressing (page 189) to coat each
onion slice. Serve garnished with fresh watercress and surrounded with slices of cold potatoes previously dipped in the
dressing.

PASTRY, CAKES, BISCUITS AND SWEETS
I DOLCI

SWEET ALMOND BISCUITS
AMARETTI

8 oz. ground almonds	1 beaten egg
2 oz. flour	1 teaspoon grated lemon rind
3 oz. castor sugar	2 teaspoons lemon juice

Pound the almonds with the sugar until fine, then mix with the flour and the lemon rind. Beat the egg and lemon juice together and stir into the almond mixture. Knead to a paste. Add more egg if necessary as the paste should not be too firm. Form into small round balls and place on a greased baking sheet and bake in a warm oven until the biscuits are brown and crisp.

'DEAD MEN'S BEANS'
FAVE DEI MORTI

These morbidly-named cakes are popular throughout Italy, and are eaten traditionally on All Souls' Day, November 2nd. Their origin is somewhat obscure, and recipes for them are to be found in all parts of Italy. In many countries, in more ancient times, beans were connected with death and with the souls of the departed. Despite their origin and name these 'beans' are extremely pleasant and the two recipes I have chosen from a dozen or more are probably two of the most simple.

RECIPE I. Cream two ounces of butter with two ounces of

166

sugar. Add one egg and continue beating until the mixture is smooth. Gradually work in eight ounces of flour and one coffee-spoonful of baking powder. Add a sherry glass of rum and enough cold water to make a stiff dough. Roll on to a floured board to a thickness of about half an inch. Cut off small pieces and shape these into beans. Brush each lightly with beaten egg and bake in a moderate oven until a golden brown.

RECIPE 2. Pound four ounces of blanched and ground almonds with four ounces of sugar until fine. Add six ounces of sieved flour. Rub in well one ounce of butter, then add one beaten egg and enough brandy and water to make a firm dough. Shape as above into beans, brush with beaten egg and bake until a golden brown in a moderate oven.

SWEET BRIOCHE
PANETTONE DI MILANO

This sweet brioche is a speciality of Milan, and owes its name to its history. The first Panettone was said to have been made by a baker called Toni. It became very popular but it had no special name, so purchasers simply asked for Panettone —Toni's bread. To enjoy it thoroughly one should, of course, sit outside a Milan café eating Panettone hot and crisp and sipping with it a glass of white wine.

¼ lb. flour	2 oz. candied peel
¼ oz. dried yeast	Rind of one lemon
2 ozs. butter	2 oz. sugar
3 egg yolks	Salt
3 ozs. raisins	¼ pint milk

Chop the peel very finely. Warm the milk, add the butter and yeast, stir until smooth and leave to rise for twenty minutes.

Sieve half the flour into a bowl, add the eggs, sugar and salt, mix well, then beat thoroughly. Add the remaining flour, the yeast mixture, the raisins, peel, lemon rind and mix everything together. Knead to a firm dough. This you must do for at least five minutes, then leave covered with a cloth for about two hours. Butter some patty tins, divide the dough into pieces, half fill each tin, and then leave until the dough has risen to twice its original size. Brush with beaten egg. Put the tins into a hot oven, and leave them for ten minutes by which time they will have started to change colour. Lower the heat to just moderate and leave for another twenty m nutes.

This recipe for Panettone is one of the simplest. 'Toni' obviously allowed variations in his bread, for some of the recipes tell you to use as many as eight eggs.

ITALIAN CHEESE CAKE
TORTA DI RICOTTA

Make enough short pastry to line a nine-inch flan tin. When mixing the pastry add sherry as well as water. It is not necessary to bake it blind first.

Short pastry (page 181)	1 *tablespoon currants*
1 *lb. cottage cheese*	1 *teaspoon vanilla essence*
1 *tablespoon chopped candied peel*	3 *eggs*
	4 *oz. sugar*

Beat the cheese vigorously with a wooden spoon until creamy. Whisk the eggs until they are frothy, add the sugar and the vanilla essence, then beat into the cheese. Continue beating until these ingredients are well blended, adding as you beat, the currants and the peel.

Fill the flan case with the cheese mixture. Bake in a very hot oven for ten minutes, then reduce the heat to moderate and bake for another thirty minutes or until the cheese filling is set. Turn off the heat, open the oven door and leave the flan there for about an hour. It should be quite cold before cutting.

SICILIAN CHEESE CAKE
CASSATA ALLA SICILIANA

1 *ten-inch round spongecake*
1 *lb. cottage cheese*
4 *oz. sugar*

4 *oz. bitter chocolate, grated*
2 *tablespoons maraschino*
2 *oz. glazed fruit*

Beat the cheese (using a wooden spoon), until it is light and feathery, then rub it through a fine sieve to make it even more so. Add the sugar, the chocolate, the maraschino and half of the fruit, previously chopped. Continue to beat until the mixture is creamy.

Cut the spongecake into three layers. Spread the creamed cheese thickly between the layers, but not on the top. This should be sprinkled only with vanilla sugar and decorated with the remaining fruit. Chill before serving.

For the spongecake, the recipe for *Pan di Spagna* (page 173) is suitable.

CATS' TONGUES
LINGUE DI GATTO

3 *oz. flour*
1 *oz. butter*
3 *oz. vanilla sugar*

3 *egg whites*
Lemon juice

Beat the butter and the sugar to a white cream, add the egg whites, stiffly beaten, then gradually add the flour and a few drops of lemon juice.

Butter a baking sheet and force the mixture through a pastry tube on to the baking sheet, leaving plenty of room between each tongue to allow the mixture to spread. Bake in a cool oven until the edges begin to turn a golden brown.

These are delicious with stewed fruit, ice cream or mousse.

CHESTNUT FLOUR CAKE
CASTAGNACCIO

Mix together five ounces of chestnut flour, a pinch of salt and two tablespoonfuls of almond oil. Blend well and stir in just enough boiling water to make a pouring consistency. Pour into a buttered, square, flat tin and sprinkle generously with pine nuts, sultanas, raisins and rosemary. This latter ingredient is most important as its flavour is characteristic of the *Castagnaccio*.

Bake in a moderate oven for three-quarters of an hour, by which time the cake should be rather crumbly. Almonds may be used if pine nuts are not available.

Chestnut flour is usually available in continental food stores.

EASTER CAKE
PRESNITZ

This quite delicious pastry originates from Castagnevizza, but has been adopted by the inhabitants of Trieste as their own.

8 oz. *puff pastry*	2 oz. *stale sponge cake*
3 oz. *sultanas*	1 *breakfast cup rum*
3 oz. *mixed nuts*	1 *egg*
2 oz. *candied peel*	½ oz. *butter*
3 oz. *Malaga raisins*	*Lemon*
2 oz. *sugar*	*Cinnamon*

Make the pastry according to any recipe you prefer as long as it is light. The Italian method of making puff pastry is the same as our own.

Stone the raisins and soak them with the sultanas in rum until they are completely round and smooth. Crumble the sponge cake into fine crumbs, coarsely grind the nuts, chop the peel and mix all these ingredients together, finally adding the rum-soaked fruit and any remaining rum. Stir until all the rum is absorbed, and add a squeeze of lemon juice and the sugar.

Roll out the pastry in a strip three inches wide and half an inch thick. Cover it with the rum-soaked mixture. Beat the egg and the butter together until smooth and then brush this over the top. Sprinkle very lightly with ground cinnamon, place on a flat buttered baking sheet, and bake in a hot oven until the pastry is a golden brown. Serve very fresh, either hot or cold. It is best eaten the day it is made.

ITALIAN RUM CAKE
ZUPPA INGLESE

Zuppa, literally, means soup, but this sweet is anything but soup-like. It is based on the English trifle or tipsy cake but is, in my opinion, very much better.

1 *lb. sponge cake*
Zabaione cream (page 187)
1 *cup rum*

Whipped cream—about ½ pint
Glazed fruits

Cut the sponge cake into three layers. Put the bottom layer on the dish in which you are going to serve the sweet. Pour over it one-third of a cup of rum and then spread it thickly with *Zabaione* cream. Add the second layer and repeat the process. Cover with the third layer, and pour the remaining rum over it but no cream.

Put the cake into the refrigerator until ready to serve. Spread thickly whipped cream over the top and sides and garnish with chopped glazed fruits before serving.

It should be firm and should cut like a layer cake.

PARADISE CAKE
TORTA PARADISO

A favourite cake with Italians and one that their cooks seem to make with ease. It is usually served simply sprinkled with vanilla sugar, but occasionally cut into layers and filled with cream.

5 eggs	1 tablespoon lemon juice
5 oz. sugar	3 oz. flour

Separate the whites from the yolks of the eggs. Beat the yolks vigorously with the lemon juice and sugar, using a fairly large bowl. Place the bowl over a saucepan of boiling water, and gently cook, stirring all the while until the mixture thickens. Leave to cool.

Beat the whites until they are stiff then fold them into the creamed yolks. Gradually add the flour, doing this carefully, and when the cake mixture is well blended pour into a greased and floured spongecake tin and bake in a moderate oven until a light brown. Leave the cake in the tin until cool.

MARGARET CAKE
TORTA MARGHERITA

5 oz. potato flour	1 teaspoon vanilla sugar
5 oz. castor sugar	1 teaspoon lemon sugar
4 eggs	

Separate the eggs and beat the yolks with the sugar. If you have the strength beat for thirty minutes! Gradually add the flour and continue beating until the mixture is very smooth. Whisk the egg whites until stiff, but not dry, and then fold them into the cake mixture. Pour this into a buttered and floured cake tin.

Bake the cake for five minutes in a very hot oven, half remove it from the oven and very quickly make a cross on the top of it. Return it to the oven and bake it in the same heat for another five minutes. Then reduce the heat to moderate and continue to bake for another thirty minutes or until the cake is cooked through.

Do not take the cake from the tin until it is quite cold. Serve it either sprinkled with vanilla or lemon sugar, or spread with fresh cream and nuts. This type of cake is garnished very much as the individual cook fancies, although the basic cake is always made in the same way.

SPONGE CAKE

PAN DI SPAGNA

4 oz. flour   1 teaspoon almond flavouring
4 eggs   1 teaspoon grated lemon rind
4 oz. castor sugar

Sift the flour three times. Separate the eggs, and beat the yolks and three ounces of the sugar together until smooth. Add the lemon rind and the flavouring.

Beat the whites until fairly stiff, add the rest of the sugar, and continue beating to a meringue consistency.

Gradually add the flour to the egg yolks, beating vigorously all the time, then fold in the egg whites. Pour mixture into a well-buttered spongecake tin and bake for about three-quarters of an hour in a moderate oven. Leave to cool in the tin.

CHESTNUT FLAN
'FLAN' DI CASTAGNE

Line a flan tin with short pastry and bake blind for ten minutes.

Roast two pounds of chestnuts for about fifteen minutes, having made a slit in their shells. Remove the outer shell and inner skin, then put into a pan with a small glass of milk, four ounces of sugar and a little vanilla essence. Cook gently until soft. Press through a ricer then beat two or three egg yolks vigorously into them. Pile this mixture into the flan case and cover with meringue, made from three egg whites and three ounces of sugar. Bake in a moderate oven until the meringue is just lightly browned.

PRUNE FLAN
BUDINO DI PRUGNE

This is a wonderful way of preparing prunes and one which makes a delicious sweet.

8 oz. short pastry	2 oz. sugar
10 oz. prunes, soaked	4 oz. stale cake crumbs
3 oz. mixed dried fruits (sultanas, currants, raisins, etc.)	2 tablespoons cream
	1 tablespoon grated lemon rind
3 oz. mixed ground nuts	1 sherry glass brandy

Line a flan tin with pastry—preferably Italian short pastry (page 181). Cook the prunes gently until very soft in a little water, adding, just before they are ready, the dried fruit. Drain, stone and chop finely. Mix with the remaining ingredients. Cool, then put into the flan case. Flute the edges, sprinkle some nuts or crumbs on the top and bake in a hottish oven for about thirty minutes, or until the pastry is a golden brown. Serve either hot or cold.

FRIED LOVERS'-KNOTS
CENCI

½ lb. flour
1 oz. butter
2 oz. castor sugar

1 whole egg plus one yolk
Egg-cup brandy

Sieve the flour and rub in the butter. Add the remaining ingredients and work the mixture to a rather stiff but very pliable dough.

Leave for half an hour wrapped in a cloth in a cool place. Roll out very thinly—almost to paper thinness—then cut into long, ribbon-like strips. Carefully tie these into lovers'-knots and quickly fry them in deep, boiling-hot fat until they are a golden brown.

Spread the *Cenci* on absorbent paper to drain away excess fat, sprinkle with castor sugar and serve hot, either alone or with fruit salad, cold mousse or a similar type of sweet.

BATTER FRITTERS
LE CASTAGNOLE

1 whole egg
Flour
Sugar

Grated Lemon rind
Salt
Oil

Many Italian provinces claim these delicious batter fritters as their own invention. Certainly they are easily obtained in Rome.

Exact amounts for the ingredients cannot be given, but, even so, the fritters are easy enough to prepare.

Beat the egg in a large bowl with one dessertspoonful of fine sugar, about one tablespoonful of oil, and a pinch of salt and

lemon rind to flavour. When these ingredients are thoroughly blended, add enough sieved flour to make a paste of 'dropping' consistency. Work this until it is almost velvety in texture.

Have ready a pan with plenty of boiling hot oil and drop the paste into this in spoonfuls—not too many at a time as the fritters will swell. Fry them until they are a golden brown, then take them out with a perforated spoon and place them on absorbent paper to drain off the surplus fat. Sprinkle with castor sugar and lemon juice and serve as hot as possible. Sometimes *Le Castagnole* are served with a thin jam or chocolate sauce.

CHESTNUT FRITTERS
FRITTELLE DI CASTAGNE

Prepare a chestnut purée as for a chestnut flan (page 174), and leave it to become very cold. A few hours in the refrigerator is ideal. Break off pieces about the size of a walnut and shape into balls. Roll in beaten egg and breadcrumbs and fry in deep fat until brown. Drain off excess fat on absorbent paper, sprinkle the fritters with vanilla sugar and serve hot. Sometimes these fritters are served with a thin chocolate sauce.

APPLE FRITTERS
FRITTELLE DI MELE

Make a coating batter (page 187).

Peel and core three or four large cooking apples, and cut them into thick slices. Rub each slice with lemon, sprinkle generously with castor sugar and leave to soak for about half an hour in rum or brandy. Dip each slice into the batter and fry in deep, boiling fat until a pale amber colour. Drain off

excess fat on to absorbent cooking paper, sprinkle with vanilla sugar and serve at once.

SWEET FRIED PASTRY BALLS
ZEPPOLE ALLA NAPOLETANA

4 oz. flour	Oil
½ pint water	Sugar icing
1 wineglass brandy	Salt

Put the flour into a saucepan and gradually stir in the water; when well blended, add the brandy and a pinch of salt. Cook over a slow heat, stirring all the time, until the mixture comes away from the sides of the saucepan. Remove from the heat, allow to cool and then knead the dough until it is elastic and pliable.

Roll it into a long baton-like shape and cut into slices. Form each slice into a ball and fry in deep boiling oil until brown. Turn the balls from time to time so that they are equally browned all over.

Take from the pan with a perforated spoon and place on absorbent paper to drain off the excess fat. Roll in sieved icing sugar and serve hot.

These are a St Joseph's Day speciality.

HORSESHOE CRISPS
CORNETTI

Make about half a pound of rich puff pastry. Roll it out very thinly and cut it into strips. Shape the strips into horseshoes with the ends turned inside the shoe. Brush lightly with melted butter and dredge with castor sugar. Bake on a greased

7

baking sheet in a moderate oven until crisp and fairly dark brown. Take them from the oven and, while still hot, sprinkle with a little vanilla sugar. Leave until cold before serving.

They are specially good with morning coffee.

PASTRY ROLL
WITH HONEY AND NUTS
PIZZA 'FIGLIATA'

Make a rich, short pastry using eggs and sherry in the mixing. Roll it thinly, then brush with honey. Sprinkle generously with chopped mixed nuts (walnuts, almonds, hazel-nuts, etc.) and chopped candied peel. Dredge lightly with mixed cake spice and shape into a spiral.

Bake in a moderate oven for about twenty minutes. This roll is useful for morning coffee or children's teas.

ST JOSEPH'S DAY FRITTERS
FRITTELLE DI SAN GIUSEPPE

The Feast Day of St Joseph, patron saint of hearth and home, is celebrated with much eating and ceremony. In Sicily it is the tradition for the rich to give a party on this day and to invite all their less wealthy neighbours; by the same tradition, the tables should literally groan with good food. As a result, quite a number of dishes are accepted as St Joseph's Day specialities. Cheese seems to be banned on this particular Saint's day, and is not served even with the rich soups and the many *pasta* dishes that are eaten. It is made up for by many sweets.

St Joseph's Day fritters are made with rice, and you should start preparing them the day before they are to be eaten.

Cook four ounces of rice slowly in one pint of milk until the rice is very soft and has absorbed all the milk. Sweeten with sugar. Flavour with vanilla sugar or vanilla essence and one tablespoon of grated lemon rind, or orange and lemon rind mixed. Cool, then beat in two whole eggs, and two ounces of potato flour. If this type of flour is not available then ordinary white flour will do. Add one sherry glass of marsala. Leave to stand overnight or for several hours in a refrigerator then shape into croquettes. Fry in deep boiling fat until golden brown.

Serve sprinkled with sugar. The croquettes are rather better, and easier to fry, if rolled first in egg and breadcrumbs.

POOR KNIGHTS OF WINDSOR

PANORATO ALLA ROMANA

This recipe seems to turn up in every country, probably because it is easy to make, cheap to prepare and most people appear to like it.

Slices of bread   *Vanilla sugar or cinnamon*
Egg   *Lemon juice*
Milk   *Butter for frying*
Sugar

Exact amounts depend on personal needs.

Soak the bread in slightly sweetened milk for fifteen minutes. Sprinkle with lemon juice, then lay the slices carefully in beaten egg. Leave them until they have completely absorbed the egg, turning them once during the process.

Have ready a pan with melted hot butter and carefully place the bread in the pan. Fry on both sides until brown. Sprinkle with vanilla sugar or cinnamon and serve hot. The fried slices can be served alone or with stewed fruit.

Stale slices of bread are the best, cut neither too thick nor too thin and with the crusts cut off before soaking. For twelve slices of bread one needs two eggs. The finished slices should be fairly crisp on the outside but soft inside.

RICE PUDDING, ITALIAN STYLE
TORTA DI RISO

4 oz. rice
2 pints milk
1 oz. butter
1 oz. ground almonds
3 oz. sugar

3 oz. candied fruit
Vanilla essence
Pinch of salt
Grated orange peel

Boil the rice for about three minutes in two pints of water, drain and leave to cool. Bring the milk with the almonds and orange peel to the boil and throw in the rice, afterwards adding the butter and the salt. Let the milk boil quickly for ten minutes, then add the sugar and vanilla essence. Pour into a well-buttered dish and bake in a warm oven for one hour.

Decorate with candied peel before serving—and with whipped cream when this is available.

SUGAR SYRUP
SCIROPPO DI ZUCCHERO

Put half a pound of sugar into a saucepan with half a pint of cold water and bring very slowly to boiling point. Take off the scum from the top, then cover, and boil quickly for five minutes. Reduce the heat, and continue to cook, still boiling but more gently, for another twenty-five minutes. Remove from the stove and cool. The syrup may be stored for future use in glass jars.

SHORT PASTRY (ITALIAN)
PASTA FROLLA

8 oz. sieved flour	2 egg yolks
4 oz. butter	Cinnamon or grated lemon rind
3 oz. sugar	Salt

With the tips of the fingers or with a knife lightly work the
butter into the flour until it has all but disappeared. Add the
sugar, salt and cinnamon or lemon rind. Of the latter you need
only enough to give the faintest flavour. When all these ingredients are well blended, make a well in the centre, drop in
the eggs, and mix to a paste with a wooden spoon. Add enough
ice-cold water to make a firm dough, and then, if you have
time, wrap the pastry in a cloth and leave it in a refrigerator
until the next day—this will greatly improve the pastry.

This pastry is suitable for sweet tarts, pies, flans, etc. When
making tarts the Italians use their imagination, putting in
plenty of fruit and cream, nuts and flavouring.

ST JOSEPH'S PUFFS
SFENCI DI SAN GIUSEPPE

6 oz. flour	1 teaspoon grated lemon rind
3 oz. butter	1 teaspoon grated orange rind
3 eggs	Salt
½ pint water	Cheese filling
1 teaspoon baking powder	

Sift the flour twice. Put the water, butter and a pinch of salt
into a saucepan and bring slowly to the boil stirring all the
time. Add all the flour at once, still stirring, then remove the
mixture from the heat and beat vigorously. Lower the heat and
continue to cook slowly, stirring all the time, until the mixture

comes away from the sides of the pan. Leave to cool until it is just warm.

Separate the eggs and add the yolks one by one to the paste beating each in thoroughly. Add the baking powder, grated orange and lemon rind, and finally the egg whites, beaten very stiff. Drop the mixture in tablespoonfuls on to a greased baking sheet and bake first for ten minutes in a very hot oven, then for about thirty minutes in a moderate oven until the puffs are a delicate golden brown.

Immediately upon taking them from the oven open them up through the centre to allow the steam to escape. Cool and fill with a cheese filling exactly similar to that used in *Cassata alla Siciliana* (page 169).

BAKED APPLES
MELE AL FORNO

Scoop out the centres of as many large and firm apples as required. Sprinkle the insides with sugar, and push into each a stick of bitter chocolate leaving about half an inch of it showing above the apples. Pour over them some marsala, and bake in a moderate oven until the apples are cooked through, basting from time to time with marsala.

STUFFED DATES
DATTERI FARCITI

Dates fresh from the trees are, of course, ideal for this recipe, but as these are usually difficult to obtain, good quality boxed dates can be used. Stone them with care and stuff them with the following mixture.

Pound three or four ounces of pistachio nuts in a mortar

with two ounces of sugar. Moisten with sherry, brandy or rum,
and work to a soft paste, like almond paste. Fill each date with
some of this filling. It should be enough for about two dozen
large dates. Garnish each date with half a blanched walnut.

BRANDIED CHESTNUTS
CASTAGNE ALLA FIAMMA

Bake one pound of large chestnuts until they can be peeled
with ease. Make about one cup of sugar syrup (page 180) and
simmer the chestnuts in this until the syrup is completely
absorbed.

Arrange the chestnuts in a silver serving dish, pour some
warmed and really good brandy over them and set them alight
just before serving.

CHESTNUT PUREE
WITH COFFEE CREAM
DOLCE DI CASTAGNE

Make some chestnut purée (page 174), but mix some well-
flavoured liqueur with it. Cherry brandy or maraschino is the
Italian choice. Pile the purée into champagne glasses or glasses
of a similar type and cover with coffee cream.

COFFEE CREAM

1 *pint milk*	2 *egg whites*
1 *teaspoon cornflour*	4 *oz. sugar*
¼ *pint strong black coffee*	*Vanilla essence*
2 *egg yolks*	*Grated chocolate*

Take a little of the milk and mix it with the cornflour to a thin paste. Strain the coffee through a cloth and mix with the remaining milk.

Bring the coffee-milk to the boil, add the cornflour and cook slowly for five minutes, stirring all the while. Remove from the heat and leave to cool. Beat the yolks with the sugar until they are frothy and add them to the coffee cream. Beat well for a minute or two, then re-heat and cook over a double boiler until the coffee mixture thickens. Add the essence, leave to cool again, and fold in the egg whites, previously stiffly beaten. Pour this cream over the chestnuts, and sprinkle with a little grated chocolate. Serve cold.

'WHITE MOUNTAIN'
MONTEBIANCO

This happens to be one of my favourite desserts, probably because I like almost anything cooked with chestnuts, which are not appreciated in England as much as I feel they should be. The Italians have a custom of offering a bowl of hot chestnuts and a bottle of wine as an impromptu meal for the unexpected guest. They also have a charming chestnut proverb—'The chestnut is for the man who takes its shell off'.

1 *lb. chestnuts*	*Milk*
1 *cup thick whipping cream*	*4 oz. castor sugar*

Roast or boil the chestnuts until you are able to remove the outer shell and the inner skin. Return them to the pan, well cover with milk, add the sugar, and cook until they are soft enough to pass through a potato ricer or coarse wire sieve. The chestnuts should look like vermicelli after this process. Pile them into a cone shape, and then put them into the refrigerator or keep in a very cold place for several hours. Whip the cream until it is light, and just before serving the chestnuts completely cover the cone with the cream, so that the finished result is indeed a 'White Mountain'.

Usually I mix one stiffly beaten egg white in my cream simply to make it lighter.

Some cooks add grated chocolate to the chestnuts while they are cooking, and sprinkle the cone with it just before adding the cream. It is a matter of taste. For the amounts given above, four ounces of chocolate would be sufficient.

STUFFED FRESH PEACHES
PESCHE RIPIENE

6 *large ripe peaches*
3 *oz. sweet almonds*
1 *oz. toasted almonds*
8 *small macaroons*

3 *oz. sieved icing sugar*
Brandy
1 *tablespoon candied peel, finely chopped*

This is a traditional sweet from Milan.

Scald the peaches for a moment or two in boiling water then peel off their skins. Halve lengthwise, remove the stones, and scoop out a little of the pulp from each.

Grind the almonds and pound them until mealy. Mix with the sugar, the macaroons, previously crushed to fine crumbs, the peel and the scooped-out peach pulp. Moisten with brandy, and when the mixture is well blended put some into each of the peach halves. Rejoin the halves and fix with cocktail sticks. Brush with brandy and dust lightly with sieved icing sugar. Bake in a moderate oven for about twenty minutes. They are nicest when heated brandy is poured over them and then set alight, but if you serve them cold with whipped cream they will still make a dish to remember.

ORANGE BALLS
PALLOTTOLE D'ARANCIA

Peel six large, thick-skinned oranges and one lemon. Remove all pith and soak the peel in cold water for twenty-four hours. Add one teaspoonful of salt. Drain and wash thoroughly. Weigh the peel and then put it into a saucepan of cold water and bring slowly to the boil. Change the water and bring once more to the boil, then simmer until the peel is soft.

When the peel is tender drain and cut it very finely. Mix with its own weight in sugar, one ounce of which should be vanilla sugar.

Return to the saucepan and cook very slowly over a low heat for about fifteen minutes or until a small amount dropped from a spoon into cold water forms a ball.

Leave the mixture to cool, then form it into balls and roll them first in icing sugar, then in finely-ground hazel nuts.

Serve cold. They are rather good as an after-dinner sweet.

If you prefer a more bitter-sweet taste, add more lemon peel and less orange peel.

STUFFED ORANGES
ARANCE RIPIENE

Two ways of stuffing oranges:

1. Slice off the top of as many oranges as required, and carefully take out the pulp from each. Cut this into cubes, and mix it with an equal amount of fresh or frozen strawberries. Put the fruit into a bowl and flavour with brandy or kirsch to taste. Sprinkle with castor sugar and leave for several hours in a cold place. Just before you are ready to serve the oranges pack them with the fruit, and cover with whipped cream.

2. Proceed as above, but only half-fill the oranges with the mixed fruit. Add enough very firmly frozen ice cream to almost reach the top of the orange and then cover this with meringue, making quite sure that the ice cream is well insulated. Put the oranges into a very hot oven for one minute and serve at once.

EGG PUNCH
ZABAIONE

Zabaione is probably one of the best-known Italian sweets. It is served in glasses, either hot or cold, and is eaten with a spoon.

For each egg yolk you need one tablespoonful of sugar and two of marsala. Whisk the eggs until they are a very pale lemon colour. Add the sugar and marsala and whisk again until they are all well blended. Put the mixture in the top of a double boiler and cook over very hot water until it thickens. Stir constantly while cooking and do not on any account let the mixture boil, nor let the bottom of the pan touch the water.

COATING BATTER

4 oz. flour	Pinch of salt
1 beaten egg	1 teaspoon baking powder
¼ pint milk	Sugar to taste

Sieve the baking powder with the flour. Add salt, sugar and then the egg. Beat until smooth, then gradually add the milk. Add more flour if too thin for coating, more milk if too thick.

SAUCES
LE SALSE

BECHAMEL SAUCE
LA BESCIAMELLA

Recipes for this sauce vary from country to country. As far as
the Italians are concerned it should be a basic white sauce.
This is their recipe.

2 oz. butter
2 oz. sieved flour
½ pint milk

Salt and pepper
Pinch nutmeg

Melt the butter and blend in the flour. Gradually add the milk,
stirring all the time. Reduce the heat, add seasonings and nutmeg, and cook for five minutes.

BOLOGNESE SAUCE
SALSA BOLOGNESE

1 small tin tomato paste
4 oz. raw beef or bacon minced
3 oz. mushrooms, chopped
1 onion, chopped
1 tablespoon parsley, chopped

1 teaspoon sugar
Salt and pepper
1 wineglass white wine
1 pint stock
Butter and oil

Heat one tablespoonful each of butter and oil. Brown the
parsley and onion, then add the mushrooms and the beef.
Simmer for three minutes, add the wine, and continue to

simmer the mixture until the wine has evaporated. Dilute the tomato paste with the stock, add the sugar, salt and pepper and pour this over the meat. Stir everything together well, continue to simmer for another thirty minutes.

GREEN SAUCE

SALSA VERDE

Pound two cloves of garlic in a mortar to a paste and add a heaped tablespoon of finely chopped parsley, a dessertspoonful of capers, three fillets of anchovies and one small, chopped gherkin. Continue pounding until a smooth paste is achieved. Add a very little grated onion—or, better still, onion juice—and one dessertspoonful of soft white breadcrumbs. Pour in a teaspoonful of olive oil, drop by drop, then dilute with lemon juice until the mixture is fairly liquid.

A more simple version of the same sauce is to combine some finely chopped parsley, capers and anchovies with one chopped hardboiled egg. Add a vinegar and oil dressing and enough soft breadcrumbs to give body to the sauce.

ITALIAN DRESSING

SALSA

1 *clove garlic*	*Tarragon or mint*
1 *teaspoon French mustard*	*Lemon juice*
Salt, pepper, sugar	*Olive oil*

Pound the garlic until smooth. Add the mustard, salt, pepper and sugar. Stir until smooth then add, drop by drop, a little lemon juice. When this is well blended gradually work in about two tablespoonfuls of good quality olive oil and just a touch of chopped, fresh tarragon or mint.

ITALIAN SAUCE
SALSA ALL'ITALIANA

1 *heaped tablespoon of chopped parsley*	*Salt and pepper*
½ *oz. dried mushrooms*	6 *chopped shallots*
2 *oz. butter*	½ *cup stock*
1 *teaspoon tomato paste*	1 *glass sweet white wine*
	Juice of half a lemon

For an authentic flavour use Italian mushrooms and soak for thirty minutes in tepid water. Chop them finely and sauté them with the parsley in butter, stirring all the time. As they begin to change colour add the shallots, salt and pepper and then the wine. Simmer until the wine is reduced to half, then add the tomato paste previously mixed with the stock and simmer for another five minutes. Add the lemon juice and serve hot with meat.

LOBSTER SAUCE FOR SPAGHETTI
SALSA D'ARAGOSTA

1 *cooked lobster, or its tinned equivalent*	3 *tablespoons olive oil*
1 *large chopped onion*	*Parsley and basil*
1 *pint lobster stock*	2 *cloves garlic*
4 *tomatoes, peeled and chopped*	1 *oz. tin tomato paste*
	Salt and pepper

Heat the oil and fry the garlic, onion and parsley until brown. Add the tomatoes, salt, pepper and chopped basil. Simmer for several minutes, add the stock and tomato paste. Cook until the tomatoes are soft. Add lobster meat and continue simmering for fifteen minutes.

If you are using tinned lobster then strain off all the liquid in the pan and use this with boiling water to make up the pint.

BUTTER SAUCE
SALSA DI BURRO

Chop half an onion and a sprig of parsley very finely. Put both
in a pan with a wineglass of a light white wine. Simmer until
the amount of wine is reduced to one-third. Cream two ounces
of butter and gradually add it to the onion and parsley. Stir
to a creamy, light, and smooth consistency. On no account
allow the butter to brown. Season with salt and pepper.

It is best to cook this sauce either over boiling water or with
a sheet of asbestos between the flame and the pan.

ANCHOVY SAUCE
SALSA D'ACCIUGHE

Make a sauce with flour, butter and fish stock. Add a little
chopped green pepper, parsley and garlic, a few crushed capers
and ground black pepper. Mash eight anchovy fillets until soft
and stir into the sauce. Stir until the sauce is well cooked and
smooth. Serve with hot fish.

GARLIC AND ANCHOVY SAUCE
'BAGNA CAUDA'

This sauce is one of the specialities of Piedmontese cooking.

Heat four ounces of butter in an earthenware saucepan and
very slightly brown four finely chopped cloves of garlic. Add
eight pounded fillets of anchovy and stir these ingredients
together with a wooden spoon. Serve very hot.

In Piedmont, truffles, which are plentiful, are added to the
sauce.

It is usual to serve *bagna cauda* in the saucepan in which it is cooked and to serve it hot at table over a spirit lamp. Pieces of uncooked vegetables, such as globe artichokes (a favourite continental vegetable), crisp celery or endive are dipped in it.

GARLIC SAUCE
AIOLI

Pound in a mortar four cloves of garlic and a pinch of salt to a paste. Beat one yolk of egg until it is absolutely smooth and gradually add it to the pounded garlic. Add olive oil, drop by drop as for mayonnaise, until you have a thick cream. Then gradually dilute this with lemon juice, using the whole of one lemon.

LEMON SAUCE
SALSA AL LIMONE

Make a white roux with one ounce of butter and one of flour. Add enough warm milk to make a smooth white sauce. Season and cook fairly quickly for ten minutes. Remove from the fire, allow the sauce to cool slightly, then whip in two well-beaten eggs. Return the sauce to the fire and gently re-heat it. Add a tablespoonful of chopped parsley, a dessertspoonful of capers and the juice of a large, juicy lemon. Stir until all the in-gredients are well blended.

This sauce can be eaten both with hot and with cold meats.

GENOA PASTE
PESTO ALLA GENOVESE

Pound in a mortar to a smooth paste three cloves of garlic, plenty of basil, three ounces of grated Pecorino cheese and a tablespoonful of pine nuts. Add olive oil, drop by drop, and thin the paste to a cream.

Another pesto is made from pounded anchovies, garlic, basil and cheese diluted with oil.

Pesto is usually served as a sauce with *pasta* or stirred into soup.

DRIED MUSHROOM SAUCE
SALSA DI FUNGHI

Use about two tablespoonfuls of dried Italian mushrooms. Chop them fairly finely and soak them for thirty minutes in tepid water. Heat some butter, oil and bacon fat in a pan, then lightly fry one finely-chopped onion and a finely-sliced stick of celery. Stir in two tablespoonfuls of soft breadcrumbs and when all these ingredients are browned, add the mushrooms, stirring well. Add one tablespoonful of tomato paste and enough meat stock to make a sauce, and simmer for half an hour. Season with salt and pepper then serve hot with either noodles or spaghetti.

PAPRIKA SAUCE
SALSA ALLA PAPRIKA

Heat about one ounce of butter in a pan and lightly fry one or two finely-chopped spring onions, or one-third of a Spanish-type onion. Sprinkle in one ounce of flour, enough water to make a paste and stir, adding one tablespoonful of paprika—the sweet Hungarian type—salt and pepper. Still stirring, gradually add enough milk to make a sauce of a Béchamel consistency. One or two tablespoonfuls of cream beaten into the sauce is naturally a great improvement.

This sauce is good with ragouts, thick stews, risottos, and other savoury dishes.

PRUNE SAUCE
SALSA DI PRUGNE

Fry a chopped onion and two chopped rashers of bacon lightly in butter. Add a small glass of white wine and simmer until this has been reduced to half. Add about four ounces of prunes, previously soaked and stoned, salt, thyme, sugar, one or two bayleaves and cold water to cover. Cook slowly until the prunes are soft, then rub everything through a sieve. Beat until smooth, dilute with a little more wine, then gently re-heat.

SALAD DRESSING
SALSA MILANO

Combine four tablespoonfuls of olive oil with two tablespoonfuls of red wine. Add a very little basil, rubbed until powdered, a good pinch of dried mustard and a level teaspoonful of good quality anchovy paste. You will not need salt as the anchovy paste supplies enough.

SAUCE FOR OSSOBUCO
SALSA PER OSSOBUCO

Take some of the liquid from your *Ossobuco* (page 104), and put it into a small pan. Add a good handful of chopped parsley, one chopped clove of garlic, some chopped lemon rind, rosemary and sage. Season with salt and pepper. Thicken slightly with a flour and water paste and simmer gently for ten minutes. Serve hot.

SAUCE PIQUANTE
SALSA PICCANTE

Blend one cup of red wine with one cup of olive oil and one-third of a cup of wine vinegar. Add one finely-chopped onion, two chopped cloves of garlic, half a coffeespoonful of dried red pepper seeds, a pinch of rosemary and salt. Whip well together so that they are perfectly blended, then leave them in a sealed jar for twenty-four hours, before using.

This can be used either as a cold dressing for meats and fowl or as a basting mixture.

SWEET-SOUR SAUCE
SALSA AGRODOLCE

2 oz. sugar
1 clove garlic
2 bayleaves

½ cup wine vinegar
2 oz. grated chocolate
Gravy

Cook the sugar in a thick saucepan until it is a light caramel colour. Add garlic, bayleaves, vinegar and chocolate. Simmer and stir until the chocolate melts, then add enough gravy to make a sauce of pouring consistency.

To be strictly authentic, you should use a gravy from venison or hare for this sauce.

SWEET-SOUR SAUCE FOR FISH
SALSA AGRODOLCE PER PESCI LESSI

Heat one tablespoonful each of oil and butter. Fry until brown a handful of chopped parsley, a little chopped basil and one small chopped onion. Add salt, pepper, a good pinch of cinnamon and six chopped tomatoes. Stir, then add a wineglass of white wine and a heaped teaspoonful of sugar. Simmer until the tomatoes are soft.

TOMATO SAUCE
SALSA DI POMIDORO

SAUCE 1. Peel and slice one pound of tomatoes with one chopped onion, carrot, celery, thyme, parsley and basil or marjoram. Cook very gently for one hour. Rub through a sieve and season to taste. This is the simplest form of tomato sauce.

SAUCE 2. Lightly brown two ounces of chopped bacon, or ham, in a mixture of olive oil and butter. Add one finely-chopped onion, chopped parsley and thyme, one or two bay-leaves and fry until the onion is brown. Add a little flour, stir and cook until this too is brown—but take care not to burn it—then add two pounds of chopped tomatoes. Stir well and cook very gently for one hour, then rub through a sieve.

The Italians use *prosciutto,* and garlic may be added according to taste.

TOMATO SAUCE PIQUANTE
SALSA ALLA PIZZAIOLA

Chop two cloves of garlic and brown them in oil. Add four peeled and chopped tomatoes and cook them quickly. Add a good measure of chopped parsley and sweet marjoram and cook until the tomatoes are well pulped and can be rubbed through a sieve. Season with salt and pepper.

TRUFFLE SAUCE

SALSA DI TARTUFI

Although the cost of producing this sauce in Britain would be expensive, it should be on record.

Heat two ounces of butter rather slowly and lightly brown one grated onion and one clove of garlic. Stir in an ounce of flour and pour in half a glass of marsala. Continue simmering and stirring until the sauce is smooth. Season with salt and pepper, remove the garlic and add one small slivered white truffle. Continue simmering over the lowest possible heat for fifteen minutes. To be served with roast meats.

VEGETARIAN SAUCE FOR SPAGHETTI

SPAGHETTI DI MAGRO

Fry very lightly in olive oil one chopped onion, carrot, turnip, parsnip, stick of celery, two tomatoes and a large sprig of chopped parsley. Season with salt and black pepper and add one pint of hot stock. Simmer for thirty minutes.

When serving this sauce with spaghetti it is not usual to include grated cheese.

INDEX